Beginning Contract Law

Whether you're new to higher education, coming to legal study for the first time or just wondering what Contract Law is all about, **Beginning Contract Law** is the ideal introduction to help you hit the ground running. Starting with the basics and an overview of each topic, it will help you come to terms with the structure, themes and issues of the subject so that you can begin your Contract Law module with confidence.

Adopting a clear and simple approach with legal vocabulary explained in a detailed glossary, Chris Monaghan and Nicola Monaghan break the subject of Contract Law down using practical, everyday examples to make it understandable for anyone, whatever their background. Diagrams and flowcharts simplify complex issues, important cases are identified and explained and on-the-spot questions help you recognise potential issues or debates within the law so that you can contribute in classes with confidence.

Beginning Contract Law is an ideal first introduction to the subject for LLB, GDL or ILEX students, and especially international students, those enrolled on distance-learning courses or on other degree programmes.

Chris Monaghan is a Lecturer in Law at BPP University College in London.

Nicola Monaghan is a Barrister and Senior Tutor in Law at Coventry University London Campus.

Beginning the Law

A new introductory series designed to help you master the basics and progress with confidence.

Publishing Spring 2013:

Following in Spring 2014:

www.routledge.com/cw/beginningthelaw

Beginning Contract Law

CHRIS MONAGHAN
and
NICOLA MONAGHAN

Routledge
Taylor & Francis Group

LONDON AND NEW YORK

First published 2013
by Routledge
2 Park Square, Milton Park, Abingdon, Oxon OX14 4RN

Simultaneously published in the USA and Canada
by Routledge
711 Third Avenue, New York, NY 10017

Routledge is an imprint of the Taylor & Francis Group, an informa business

British Library Cataloguing in Publication Data
A catalogue record for this book is available from the British Library

Library of Congress Cataloging in Publication Data
A catalog record for this book has been requested.

ISBN: 978–0–415–52377–6 (hbk)
ISBN: 978–0–415–52376–9 (pbk)
ISBN: 978–0–203–56921–4 (ebk)

Typeset in Vectora LH
by RefineCatch Limited, Bungay, Suffolk

Printed and bound in Great Britain by
TJ International Ltd, Padstow, Cornwall

Contents

Table of Cases

Table of Legislation

Preface

Contract law is an interesting subject that is relevant to each of our daily lives as most people will enter into contracts on a daily basis. Whether you are negotiating high-value contracts in a business setting, starting a new job and contracting with an employer, taking out a loan, or simply buying a train ticket or entering into a contract for sale as a consumer, the general principles of contract law will apply to your transaction.

Beginning Contract Law is designed to give you a basic understanding of the law of contract and to introduce you to key concepts and principles of law. The law of contract is fundamental to any legal studies, and indeed, business studies. Both lawyers and those operating in a business environment need to have at least a basic understanding of matters such as how a contract is formed, the implications of making false statements during contractual negotiations, the validity of specific types of clauses such as exclusion or limitation clauses and penalty clauses, and an appreciation of the available remedies should the other party fail to perform their contractual obligations.

This book is intended to supplement your studies and make these topics accessible through the use of key features such as diagrams, key case analysis boxes, key definitions and on-the-spot questions to test your own understanding of the subject. We have also compiled an annotated further reading list to help you develop a deeper awareness of key legal debates and issues, and the online resource centre attached to this book provides further resources, such as a glossary of key terms used.

We would like to take the opportunity to express our gratitude to our editors, Damian Mitchell and Fiona Briden at Routledge, for their invaluable support, encouragement and guidance throughout the writing process. We would also like to thank those at Routledge who were involved in the production process and the anonymous academic reviewers. Finally, we would like to dedicate this book to our respective parents, Michael and Marie, and Nick and June.

Any errors or omissions in the text are entirely ours. The law is as stated on 1 September 2012.

Chris Monaghan   Nicola Monaghan
BPP University College, London   Coventry University London Campus

September 2012

Guide to the Companion Website

www.routledge.com/cw/beginningthelaw

Visit the *Beginning the Law* website to discover a comprehensive range of resources designed to enhance your learning experience.

Answers to on-the-spot-questions
Podcasts from the authors provide pointers and advice on how to answer the on-the-spot questions in the book.

Online glossary
Reinforce your legal vocabulary with our online glossary flashcards. The flashcards can be used online, or downloaded for reference on the go. Key terms are emboldened throughout the book, and you will find a deck of simple and easy-to-understand definitions of all these terms for each chapter of the book here.

Case flashcards

Test your knowledge of the key cases with this deck of flashcards that could be used to identify either the case name from the precedent set or the precedent from the case name. The flashcards can be used online or downloaded for revision on the go.

Weblinks

Discover more with this set of online links to sources of further interest. These include links to contemporary news stories, editorials and articles, illuminating key issues in the text.

Updates

Twice a year, our authors provide you with updates of the latest cases, articles and debates within the law, so you can be confident you will always be on track with the very latest developments.

Chapter 1
An introduction to contract law

VERY BRIEF GUIDE TO CONTRACT LAW

Contract law is a very logical subject which is based upon the principle of freedom of contract. This principle provides that parties to a contract are generally free to contract with whomever they wish and about whatever they want. The law and the courts aim not to interfere with this freedom unless it is absolutely necessary to do so.

In this book we will look at the formation of a contract and the elements required for a contract to exist, which are: offer, acceptance, consideration, capacity and the intention to create legal relations. Then we shall look at the contents of a contract and express and implied contractual terms. We will consider how terms, including exclusion clauses and limitation clauses, are incorporated into a contract and the validity of such exemption clauses. We will explore the classification of terms as conditions, warranties and innominate terms, and the effect of this upon breach of contract. We will see the effect of vitiating factors such as misrepresentation, mistake, duress and undue influence upon the contract. Consideration will be given to whether a person who is not a party to the contract can sue or be sued upon the contract in the chapter on privity of contract. Finally, we will look at the different ways in which a contract can be discharged (by agreement, performance, breach and frustration) and the remedies available for breach of contract.

This book will give you a basic understanding of the main areas of contract law and the key cases and principles. The book aims to introduce key principles to you and provide you with a solid foundation in contract law that you can then build upon by reading more academic textbooks and journal articles.

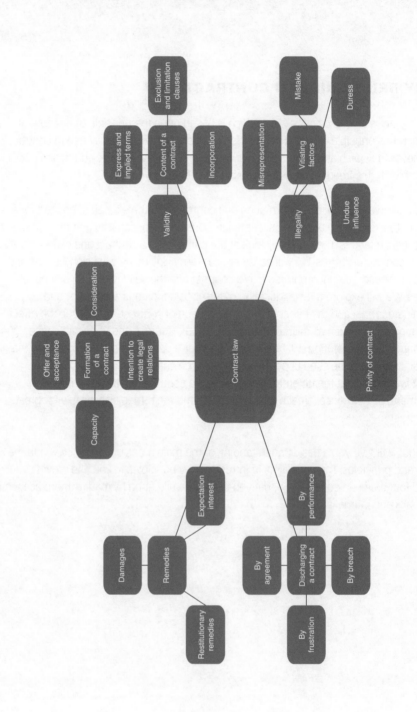

BASIC STUDY SKILLS FOR CONTRACT LAW

Case law

Contract law is predominantly a case law based subject; much of contract law has been created by the courts. This means that although there are some statutes that you will be required to read in studying this subject, the main part of your learning will centre on case law. This book helps you to identify the key cases in contract law and the legal principles from those cases. During your studies, you will need to obtain a more detailed understanding of the subject and this is best gained by reading the original case reports. These are available online or in hardcopy in your university library. Cases can appear confusing because the language used may be outdated, or there could be a number of judges giving their own reasons for the decision. It is important that you search through the report of the case to find the judgments and that you read these in full. If you require help, there are case commentaries written by academics that will help to explain the case.

Students often think that knowing everything about the facts of a particular case is essential. Often the facts are important but only to explain the legal principle and why a case was distinguished from previous cases. In an exam you will be expected to apply the law, which will require knowing which case is the authority for a certain legal principle and how it relates to the facts of a problem question.

Statute

More recently, there has been an increasing number of statutes in contract law and these are often reforming the law (e.g. the Law Reform (Frustrated Contracts) Act 1943 which reformed the law on the financial implications of frustration) or providing exceptions to the common law (e.g. the Contracts (Rights of Third Parties) Act 1999 which provided a statutory exception to the doctrine of privity of contract. Statute also provides for causes of action (the Misrepresentation Act 1967 makes it easier for the claimant to establish there has been a misrepresentation and improves the remedies available) and restricts the parties' freedom of contract (the Unfair Contract Terms Act 1977 controls the use of exclusion and limitation clauses). Once again, the statute can be found online or in hardcopy and it is essential that you have read the relevant provisions. Where there is a statute, the courts will be tasked with interpreting the provisions and applying the statute to a particular set of facts. The older the statute, the more cases there will be interpreting it. You will need to remember that the courts are not allowed to ignore what Parliament intended when passing the statute, nor can they ignore precedent (the decision of a higher court).

Answering questions on contract law

In contract law, there are two types of question that you may be asked to answer. The first of these is a problem question. The purpose of a problem question is to test your knowledge of the law and your ability to apply the law to the facts. In order to do well, it is vital that you answer the question rather than writing everything you know on a particular topic as this is not what the examiner – or the client seeking your advice – is looking for. Topics that commonly appear in problem questions include offer and acceptance, misrepresentation, terms and exclusion clauses and frustration, amongst others.

An essay question tests different skills to a problem question. An essay question may ask you to analyse the law. For example, you might be asked 'Do you agree with the decision in X?', or 'Has X reformed the law on Y?' These types of questions require you to demonstrate not only good knowledge of the law, but also to critique case law and legislation with reference to academic journal articles. Examples of topics that might be examined in the form of an essay include mistake (e.g. an essay question could easily be asked on the distinction drawn by the courts between face-to-face negotiations and negotiations at a distance in relation to mistake as to identity), privity of contract and the exceptions to this, undue influence and consideration, amongst others.

For a clearer idea of the types of questions that you might be asked in an exam, refer to your institution's previous exam papers for contract law.

KEY SOURCES

Your university might have access to online electronic databases such as Westlaw, Lexis Library or Lawtel. These databases provide access to case law, statutes, e-books and journal articles. Some law firms have access to these and so you will be expected to be able to use these in practice. It is also important to be able to use hardcopy resources, such as law reports and journal articles, which can be found in your university library. Some law firms rely heavily on hardcopy resources so you must know how to use them.

Journal articles are a good way of researching the law and learning about the significance of key cases. We recommend that you look at these journals as part of your studies:

- Journal of Contract Law
- Journal of Business Law
- Modern Law Review
- Law Quarterly Review
- Cambridge Law Journal

Additionally, there are a good range of textbooks that can be used alongside your university set text.

There are some useful websites that can be accessed without payment, including:

- http://www.legislation.gov.uk/ – this website provides access to all United Kingdom legislation.
- http://www.bailii.org/ – this website provides access to key cases.

Chapter 2
Elements of a contract I

LEARNING OUTCOMES

After reading this chapter, you should be able to:

- Distinguish between an invitation to treat and an offer
- Understand the difference between unilateral and bilateral offers
- Appreciate the rules relating to communication of acceptance
- Understand the effect of a counter-offer or request for further information
- Demonstrate knowledge of the rules relating to revocation of an offer

INTRODUCTION

Agreement between the parties is essential to the formation of a contract. A contract places legal obligations on both parties. If we consider a contract for the sale of a Ford Mondeo in which party A will pay £25,000 to party B, in return for which B will provide a Ford Mondeo. If either A or B do not perform their obligation, they can be sued for breach of contract. Whether there will be a contract will also depend on the other elements being present: consideration, capacity and the intention to create legal relations (these will be dealt with in chapter 3). The parties must both know what they are agreeing to. There can be no difference between what A **offers** B, and what B **accepts** in return for the Ford Mondeo.

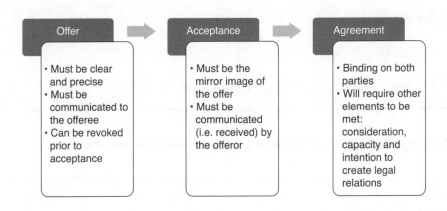

THE OFFER

The first step in reaching an agreement is the making of an offer. The offer must be clear and precise. It must be clear that the offeror (i.e. the person making the offer) intended for his statement to constitute an offer, which, if accepted by the offeree, would constitute a binding agreement. This means that the offer must be sufficiently certain and capable of being binding on the offeror.

Key Definitions

Offeror – The person making the offer.
Offeree – The person to whom the offer is made.

Unilateral offers

Where there is an exchange of promises by the parties, this is a bilateral contract. A offers to do X in return for B doing Y; B then accepts A's offer and, in doing so, agrees to do Y. By contrast, a unilateral offer is one that is made by the offeror to the world. Imagine if you lost your pet dog. You would make posters and distribute these across your neighbourhood. These posters might contain an offer to pay £200 to anyone who finds your dog. At this stage, no one has accepted your offer and no one needs to. The offer will be accepted by anyone who performs the required act (namely, finding your dog). Therefore, if someone performs the act then they accept your offer through their performance of that act.

Key Definitions

Bilateral offer – A promise made in exchange for another promise – where one party promises to perform an act in exchange for a promise from the other party to perform another act.

Unilateral offer – A promise made in exchange for performance of an act.

Distinguishing an offer from an invitation to treat

It is important to be able to distinguish an offer from an invitation to treat. An offer can be accepted and will form a legally binding agreement, whereas an invitation to treat will not. An invitation to treat is merely an invitation to parties to make an offer themselves, which can then either be accepted or rejected by the maker of the invitation to treat. An offer is final and certain, and there is no further need for negotiation, whereas an invitation to treat is seeking business and is inviting parties to negotiate with you.

Imagine that you own a shop and have just purchased a limited stock of new tablet computers. You decide to put an advert in the local newspaper informing customers that you have the tablets on sale at £100 per unit. Then you display the goods in your shop window to attract passing custom, with the remaining stock displayed inside your store. Will any of these actions amount to an offer? If these amount to offers, customers would be able to accept your offer by informing you that they wished to purchase a tablet computer for £100, and you would be bound to sell tablet computers to each of the customers at £100 per unit. Under these circumstances, you would still be bound to sell tablet computers to the customers if you ran out of stock or wished to change your mind. We will now consider whether advertisements and displays of goods amount to offers or invitations to treat.

Advertisements

KEY CASE ANALYSIS: *Partridge v Crittenden* [1968] 1 WLR 1204

Background

The defendant was prosecuted for unlawfully offering a bramblefinch hen for sale (having placed an advert in a trade magazine). This amounted to a criminal offence under s 6, Protection of Birds Act 1954. He was convicted at first instance and his conviction was quashed on appeal.

Principle established

The court ruled that placing the advert was an invitation to treat and did not amount to an offer; therefore he was not 'offering for sale' the prohibited bird as required for criminal liability under the 1954 Act.

The court in *Partridge v Crittenden* [1968] 1 WLR 1204 made reference to the judgment of Lord Herschell in *Grainger & Son v William Lane Gough (Surveyor of Taxes)* [1896] AC 325 in which the House of Lords had held that a price list did not amount to an offer. Rather, an order would need to be received (the offer) before the seller could accept it. The price list was not an offer that could be accepted by placing an order; instead, it merely constituted an invitation to treat. Lord Herschell in *Grainger* was concerned that if the price list were to be regarded as an offer, then the supplier would be bound to supply every order that was placed. Lord Herschell stated:

> The transmission of such a price-list does not amount to an offer to supply
> an unlimited quantity of the wine described at the price named, so that as
> soon as an order is given there is a binding contract to supply that quantity.
> If it were so, the merchant might find himself involved in any number of contractual
> obligations to supply wine of a particular description which he would be
> quite unable to carry out, his stock of wine of that description being necessarily
> limited.

As Lord Herschell points out, the problem with regarding the price list as an offer is that an uncertain amount of customers could accept and the supplier might not have enough stock to fulfil all the contracts made with him. So, he will not necessarily always be able to honour every order and, consequently, could find himself in breach of contract. As a result, the price list must be treated as an invitation to treat.

In *Partridge v Crittenden*, Lord Parker CJ stated *obiter* that 'There is business sense in construing advertisements and circulars, unless they come from manufacturers, as invitations to treat and not offers for sale.' Thus, Lord Parker CJ draws a distinction between sellers and manufacturers. This makes sense because a manufacturer is more likely to be able to honour orders since they have control over the production of the goods, although it is important to remember that even manufacturers might be reliant upon another party for raw materials. Consequently, every case must be determined on its own facts.

Interestingly, many of these cases involved criminal offences and it may be surprising that the cases are not reported as *R v Crittenden*, etc. The reason for this is that until the creation of the Crown Prosecution Service in 1986, criminal proceedings were brought by police officers.

KEY CASE ANALYSIS: *Carlill v Carbolic Smoke Ball Co* [1893] 1 QB 256

Background

A company had placed an advert informing potential customers that if you purchased their smoke ball and used it as prescribed, you would not catch influenza. To show their seriousness, the company stated that they would pay £100 to anyone who caught influenza. A total of £1,000 was held on account in a bank as security. The claimant purchased the smoke ball and used it in the prescribed way. She then caught influenza and sought to recover the money. The issue that arose was whether the advert was an offer or an invitation to treat.

Principle established

In *Carlill* the advert was construed as a unilateral offer. It was held that the terms contained in the advert were sufficiently precise and the customer could understand what they needed to do to accept these, thus they constituted an offer. The fact that the defendants had placed £1,000 in the bank demonstrated their intention to be bound by the advert.

The Court of Appeal supported the decision with reference to *Williams v Carwardine* (1833) 4 B & Ad 621. In that case, an advert offering a reward for information about a murder was held to amount to an offer. In *Carlill v Carbolic Smoke Ball Co*, Lindley LJ stated:

> In point of law this advertisement is an offer to pay 100l. to anybody who will perform these conditions, and the performance of the conditions is the acceptance of the offer. That rests upon a string of authorities, the earliest of which is *Williams v Carwardine*, which has been followed by many other decisions upon advertisements offering rewards.

The defendants argued that an advert should not be held to be an offer because it would be made to the entire world, and an unlimited amount of people could choose to accept it. The argument was rejected by the Court of Appeal. Bowden LJ stated:

> It was also said that the contract is made with all the world – that is, with everybody; and that you cannot contract with everybody. It is not a contract made with all the world. There is the fallacy of the argument. It is an offer made to all the world; and why should not an offer be made to all the world which is to ripen into a contract with anybody who comes forward and performs the condition? It is an offer to become liable to anyone who, before it is retracted, performs the condition, and, although the offer is made to the world, the contract is made with that limited portion of the public who come forward and perform the condition on the faith of the advertisement.

Bowden LJ distinguished the present case from advertisements where there is a limited amount of stock.

> It is not like cases in which you offer to negotiate, or you issue advertisements that you have got a stock of books to sell, or houses to let, in which case there is no offer to be bound by any contract. Such advertisements are offers to negotiate – offers to receive offers – offers to chaffer, as, I think, some learned judge in one of the cases has said. If this is an offer to be bound, then it is a contract the moment the person fulfils the condition.

The American case of *Lefkowitz v Great Minneapolis Surplus Store, Inc* 86 NW 2d 689 (Minn. 1957) is interesting. A department store advertised three fur coats for sale at $1 each. They usually retailed at $100. The sale was advertised on a first-come, first-served basis. The claimant turned up and was the first customer. The defendant refused to accept his payment. He was informed that the coats were for women only. The court held the advert amounted to a unilateral offer. The trial judge distinguished an offer from an invitation to treat, 'where the offer is clear, definite, and explicit, and leaves nothing open for negotiation, it constitutes an offer, acceptance of which will complete the contract'.

Display of goods in shop windows

In *Fisher v Bell* [1961] 1 QB 394, a display of goods in a shop window was held to not amount to an offer, but rather an invitation to treat. The defendant was charged with 'offering up for sale' an offensive weapon (a flick-knife) contrary to the Restriction of Offensive Weapons Act 1959. This meant that the defendant had not 'offered' the flick-knife for sale and thus his conviction was quashed.

Display of goods in shops

KEY CASE ANALYSIS: *Pharmaceutical Society of Great Britain v Boots Cash Chemists (Southern) Ltd* [1953] 1 QB 401

Background

The defendants, Boots Cash Chemists, had a self-service system in their chemists where customers would pick up the drugs from the shelves and take them over to the cashier for payment. The law stated that the sale would need to be supervised by a chemist. Therefore, the issue in this case was who made the offer. If the display of goods in the shop constituted an offer to sell, then acceptance would potentially take place upon a customer picking up the goods and thus the sale of the drugs would not have been supervised by a chemist.

Principle established

The court held that the display of goods was only an invitation to treat and the offer was made by the customer to the cashier. Therefore, the sale was supervised by a chemist as required by law.

In *Mella v Monahan* [1961] Crim LR 175, a shop was selling obscene photographs. Each packet cost 10 shillings. It was an offence to offer up for sale the photographs under the

Obscene Publications Act 1959. The display of goods inside a shop was held to be an invitation to treat.

On-the-spot question

 Why do you think the Court of Appeal held that there was a unilateral offer in *Carlill v Carbolic Smokeball Co*? Can you distinguish this case from *Partridge v Crittenden*?

Offer must be unambiguous, clear and precise

An offer must be unambiguous, clear and precise. The offeror's statement must be final. There can be no uncertainty. If key terms are not agreed then there cannot be an offer. English contract law requires a formulaic approach – only once there is a valid offer can there possibly be acceptance. It is not enough that the parties are in agreement on *most* of the material terms, if the remaining terms are still far too uncertain.

KEY CASE ANALYSIS: *Gibson v Manchester City Corporation* **[1978] 1 WLR 520**

Background

Mr Gibson lived in a council house in Manchester. The Conservative-led Manchester City Council had intended to sell council houses to their tenants and Mr Gibson wished to purchase his house. However, this policy was reversed by Labour when they came into power. Mr Gibson had received a letter from the council stating that they 'may be' willing to sell the house to him and he argued that this constituted an offer that he had accepted, and therefore the council were bound to sell him the council house.

In the Court of Appeal, Lord Denning had held that the letter did amount to an offer and His Lordship rejected the traditional approach of establishing that there was a clear offer and acceptance in favour of looking at the correspondence between the parties as a whole and determining whether there had been an agreement on the material terms. Lord Denning stated that:

> I do not like detailed analysis on such a point. To my mind it is a mistake to think that all contracts can be analysed into the form of offer and acceptance. I know in some of the text books it has been the custom to do

> so: but, as I understand the law, there is no need to look for a strict offer and acceptance. You should look at the correspondence as a whole and at the conduct of the parties and see therefrom whether the parties have come to an agreement on everything that was material. If by their correspondence and their conduct you can see an agreement on all material terms — which was intended thenceforward to be binding — then there is a binding contract in law even though all the formalities have not been gone through.

However, the approach of the Court of Appeal and Lord Denning was rejected by the House of Lords.

Principle established

The House of Lords held that there was no contract between Mr Gibson and the council. The House held that the council had not in fact made Mr Gibson an offer because there was no clear intention to be bound. The letter from the council, which Mr Gibson claimed contained the offer, was held only to constitute an invitation to treat since the words 'may be' willing to sell only demonstrated a willingness to enter into negotiations and not an intention to be bound.

In the House of Lords, Lord Diplock stated:

> I can see no reason in the instant case for departing from the conventional approach of looking at the handful of documents relied upon as constituting the contract sued upon and seeing whether upon their true construction there is to be found in them a contractual offer by the corporation to sell the house to Mr Gibson and an acceptance of that offer by Mr Gibson. I venture to think that it was by departing from this conventional approach that the majority of the Court of Appeal was led into error.

Offer must be communicated to the offeree

The offer needs to be communicated to the offeree. The offeree cannot accept the offer in ignorance of the offer. For example, imagine that you have lost your cat. A friend sees the cat in a nearby field and returns it to you. They did not see the adverts offering a £250 reward for finding your cat. If they later demand payment, you would have a defence as the offer had not been communicated to them. Unless there has been communication of the offer to the offeree, the offeree may not accept the offer. In the Australian case of *R v Clarke* (1927) 40 CLR 227, information relating to a murder was given to the police. There was an advert offering a reward for this information. The court held that the person who gave the information could not claim the reward because he provided the information in order to clear his name, rather than in response to the offer. Although he knew of the existence of the offer, he had forgotten about it at the time that he provided the information.

Revocation of an offer

Once the offeror has made his offer and it has been communicated to the offeree, can the offeror revoke his offer? The answer is yes, the offeror can revoke the offer and the revocation will be effective if notice of the revocation actually reaches the offeree before acceptance: see *Byrne & Co v Leon Van Tienhoven & Co* (1879–80) LR 5 CPD 344.

Once the offeree has begun performance, then the offeror will be prevented from revoking the offer. In *Offord v Davies* (1862) 142 ER 1336, the court held that the offer could be revoked until the offeree acted upon it and started to part perform the required act. Erle CJ stated, '[U]ntil the condition has been at least in part fulfilled, the defendants have the power of revoking it'. (See also *Errington v Errington & Woods* [1952] 1 KB 290.) This means that if you offered Bob £100 to complete the London Marathon, then once Bob has started to perform the marathon you cannot revoke your offer. The law does not hold Bob's part performance as acceptance; rather, Bob must still perform the entire marathon, but until he finishes (or gives up) you are prevented from revoking your offer.

In *Payne v Cave* (1789) 3 TR 148, it was held that in auction sales (without reserve) the bidder can revoke his offer at any time before the auctioneer's hammer falls. The hammer falling amounts to acceptance of that offer. The auctioneer is an agent of the seller (the principal) and has the power to conclude contracts on her behalf.

Formal notice of revocation from the offeror is not always required. In *Dickinson v Dodds* (1875–76) LR 2 Ch D 463 it was held that an offer could be revoked without formal notice being communicated to the offeree. The court said that the offeree could have notice of the revocation if they knew that the offeror had done something inconsistent with their original offer, such as selling property to another party.

If you were to send your revocation by post, then the revocation must still actually reach the offeree. This is known as the receipt rule. The posting of a letter does not act as constructive communication of the revocation. In *Byrne & Co v Leon Van Tienhoven & Co* (1879–80) LR 5 CPD 344, the court held that an offer could not be revoked by posting a letter unless the letter was received before the offeree accepted the offer.

How does an offeror revoke a unilateral offer? If the Smoke Ball Company in *Carlill* wished to revoke their unilateral offer, it might prove difficult as they would not know who exactly had seen the offer and therefore who to contact in order to revoke the offer. What happens if you inform 100,000 people who did see the offer of your revocation of that offer, but then someone whom you didn't inform, having previously seen the offer, then completes the required act? Have they accepted your offer? Unilateral offers pose an interesting problem and the case of *Shuey v United States* (1875) 92 US 73 provides a solution.

KEY CASE ANALYSIS: *Shuey v United States* (1875) 92 US 73

Background

This is an American case in which the US government published a proclamation (an official notice) advertising a reward of $25,000 for the arrest of a wanted suspect hiding in Europe after the American Civil War. This was a unilateral offer to the world, which would be accepted upon performance. A similar notice was later published revoking the original unilateral offer. However, knowing nothing about the revocation, Shuey tried to claim the reward at a later date having identified where the wanted suspect was hiding.

The issue in this case was whether the unilateral offer had been revoked before acceptance or not. In particular, the court focused on the method by which revocation must take place in order to be effective.

Principle established

The court held that it was possible to revoke unilateral offers in the same way that the offer was originally made. Thus, the offeror must use the same notoriety to revoke the offer as they first used to make the original offer.

Although *Shuey* is not an English case, it is persuasive and provides a very useful guide as to how the courts in England and Wales would approach this issue.

On-the-spot question

? Fred has lost his tap shoes and puts up notices in the West End offering £50 to anyone who finds them. Fred later decides to buy another pair and so wants to revoke his offer. He removes the old notices and puts up several new notices announcing the revocation. Ginger has previously seen the offer and finds Fred's tap shoes. She is a fan of Fred and is so excited to see him that she forgets to ask for the reward.

Advise Ginger.

ACCEPTANCE

Mirror image rule

The acceptance must mirror the offer. This means that the acceptance must be a clear and unequivocal mirror image of the terms of the offer. There cannot be differences between the terms offered and those accepted. This is because there cannot be a contract where the parties are both at odds as to what they have agreed. An agreement requires a meeting of the minds (or *consensus ad idem*). If the offeree proposes new terms, then this will not constitute acceptance but may be a counter-offer.

Counter-offer or a request for further information

When considering the offer, the offeree has a number of options. Firstly, they may accept the terms offered and there will be an agreement between the parties. Secondly, they can reject the offer or allow it to lapse. Thirdly, they can make a counter-offer or see if the offeror will accept different terms. If they make a counter-offer, then according Lord Langdale MR in *Hyde v Wrench* (1840) 49 ER 132, this will kill off the original offer. The counter-offer will be treated as an offer in its own right. The offeree cannot go back and accept the original offer as this no longer exists.

However, a counter-offer must be distinguished from a request for further information, which does not kill off the original offer – the original offer remains valid (unless it is revoked). In *Stevenson, Jacques & Co v McLean* (1879–80) LR 5 QBD 346, the court held that if the offeree were to ask whether the offeror would vary the terms, then this was not a rejection of the offer. It would appear that there is a line between suggesting your own terms (a lower price) and suggesting that the terms be varied (can you go any lower?).

The battle of the forms

In business, parties will seek to contract on their own standard terms. This is because they have drafted these terms in their own interests. Where one party sends its own standard terms to another party to contract on and the second party sends back their own standard terms, the courts will need to determine on whose terms the parties have contracted. The courts have approached this issue by looking for individual offers and acts of acceptance. Each new set of standard terms amounts to a new offer. In *Butler Machine Tools Co Ltd v Ex-Cell-O Corporation (England) Ltd* [1979] 1 WLR 401, the seller had accepted the buyer's standard terms by completing a tear-off slip on the buyer's standard form and returning it to the buyers. Lord Denning MR suggested a different approach to the traditional offer and acceptance analysis and stated that, instead, the court should take an holistic view of the documents that had passed between the parties to see if they agreed on the main terms.

However, his view was a minority one and the traditional offer–acceptance analysis is generally adopted by the courts.

Must have knowledge of the offer

Returning to *R v Clarke*, the offeree must have knowledge of the offer. Acceptance in ignorance of the offer will not be valid. See section entitled 'Offer must be communicated to the offeree' above.

Must communicate acceptance to the offeror

Crucially, the offeree must communicate his acceptance to the offeror (this is known as 'the receipt rule'). Until acceptance is communicated, the offeror is free to revoke his offer. This is explained by Denning LJ in *Entores Ltd v Miles Far East Corp* [1955] 2 QB 327 where his Lordship stated, 'Suppose, for instance, that I make an offer to a man by telephone and, in the middle of his reply, the line goes "dead" so that I do not hear his words of acceptance. There is no contract at that moment. The other man may not know the precise moment when the line failed. But he will know that the telephone conversation was abruptly broken off: because people usually say something to signify the end of the conversation. If he wishes to make a contract, he must therefore get through again so as to make sure that I heard'.

Silence cannot amount to acceptance

In *Felthouse v Bindley* (1862) 11 CB (NS) 869, the nephew was selling a horse. His uncle made an offer to purchase the horse and informed the nephew that if he did not hear back from him, he would consider the horse to be his. The court held that the nephew had not accepted the uncle's offer as silence can never amount to acceptance.

Exceptions to the receipt rule

There are two exceptions to the rule that acceptance must actually be communicated. The first of these is where the acceptance is sent by post – known as the postal rule – and the second is where there is a unilateral offer.

Postal rule

Where the offeree sends his acceptance by post, the acceptance is regarded as having taken place when the letter is posted, and not when the letter actually reaches the offeror. The authority for this rule comes from the case of *Adams v Lindsell* (1818) 1 B & Ald 681. In

Household Fire & Carriage Accident Insurance Co Ltd v Grant (1878–79) LR 4 Ex D 216, the court held that if the letter was lost in the post, the acceptance would have taken place at the moment the letter was posted. This means that if I post my acceptance to you and you never actually receive my letter, then I have nevertheless accepted your offer. The court said that the post office was a neutral agent of both parties and therefore the offeree was not at fault if the letter was lost. Importantly, the offeror can expressly exclude the postal rule when he makes the offer (this is known as 'ousting the postal rule'). If the terms of the offeror are inconsistent with the operation of the postal rule, then the postal rule will not apply and acceptance will take place when the letter is actually received by the offeror. In *Holwell Securities Ltd v Hughes* [1974] 1 WLR 155, the offer was for an option to purchase land. The offer stated that there needed to be 'notice in writing to the intending vendor'. This meant that the acceptance needed to actually be received in order for it to be communicated.

The postal rule only applies to a letter accepting the offer and not a letter revoking the offer. A classic case to explain this is *Henthorn v Fraser* [1892] 2 Ch 27.

KEY CASE ANALYSIS: *Henthorn v Fraser* [1892] 2 Ch 27

Background

This case was about the application of the postal rule. The parties were using the post to conduct their business. An offer was made, which the offeree accepted by sending a letter to the offeror. According to the postal rule, the acceptance took place then. However, the offeror had sent a letter revoking his offer prior to the offeree posting the letter of acceptance. The issue that arose was whether the revocation was effective.

Principle established

The court held that the postal rule does not apply to letters revoking offers, as the revocation needs to be received in order for it to be communicated. Although the original offer had not been made by post, the court held that the postal rule could still apply, as long as it was in the contemplation of parties that post could be used (i.e. it was reasonable to do so) to communicate acceptance. Thus, the acceptance was effective and the revocation of the offer was not.

There is a lot of controversy about the use of the postal rule so it is important that the offeror understands that it could apply. The postal rule will not apply where the letter has been sent to the wrong address (see *Korbetis v Transgrain Shipping BV* [2005] EWHC 1345 (QB)), and the offeror can always stipulate that acceptance cannot be by post.

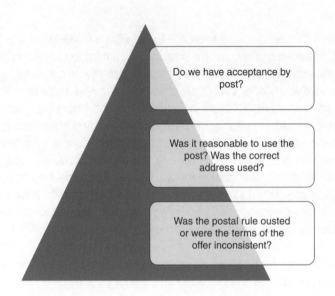

- Do we have acceptance by post?

- Was it reasonable to use the post? Was the correct address used?

- Was the postal rule ousted or were the terms of the offer inconsistent?

Does the postal rule apply to instantaneous communication?

KEY CASE ANALYSIS: *Entores Ltd v Miles Far East Corp* [1955] 2 QB 327

Background

This case concerned the use of instantaneous communications during contractual negotiations. Instantaneous communications are those such as telex (an old form of communication where the message is sent word by word), email, fax, telephone and text message. The issue that arose for consideration was whether the postal rule applies to instantaneous communications, such as telex. If the postal rule were to apply to instantaneous communications, then the contract would be concluded when the message was sent, rather than when it was received or read. This was important because the parties in this case were based in different countries and the courts had to decide where the contract was made in order to determine which country's law applied.

Principle established

The Court of Appeal held that the postal rule does not apply to instantaneous communication. Therefore, acceptance does not take place upon sending the message, but it takes place on receipt by the offeror.

Lord Denning made some interesting comments:

> In all the instances I have taken so far, the man who sends the message of acceptance knows that it has not been received or he has reason to know it. So he must repeat it. But, suppose that he does not know that his message did not get home. He thinks it has. This may happen if the listener on the telephone does not catch the words of acceptance, but nevertheless does not trouble to ask for them to be repeated: or the ink on the teleprinter fails at the receiving end, but the clerk does not ask for the message to be repeated: so that the man who sends an acceptance reasonably believes that his message has been received. The offeror in such circumstances is clearly bound, because he will be estopped from saying that he did not receive the message of acceptance. It is his own fault that he did not get it. But if there should be a case where the offeror without any fault on his part does not receive the message of acceptance – yet the sender of it reasonably believes it has got home when it has not – then I think there is no contract.

Here His Lordship states that where instantaneous methods of communication are used, the acceptance must actually reach the offeror. Where the offeror is at fault by failing to check his fax machine or voicemails, or by failing to ensure there is ink in his fax machine, then he cannot deny that the acceptance has been validly communicated. By contrast, if the message never arrives because the mobile network has crashed, etc., then it is not the offeror's fault and so the acceptance has not been communicated. In *Korbetis v Transgrain Shipping BV* [2005] EWHC 1345 (QB), the offeree attempted to accept an offer by fax; however, there was a clerical error and it was never actually received. The court held that communication had not actually taken place and the offeree should have checked to see if their acceptance had been received. In *Brinkibon Ltd v Stahag Stahl und Stahlwarenhandel GmbH* [1983] 2 AC 34, telex was used and the court held that the acceptance was communicated when it was actually received by the offeror. This was important as the contract was concluded, not when the acceptance was sent, but when it was received. This meant that the contract was made, *not* in England, but in Austria.

On-the-spot question

? Mohammed meets Sandra on Monday in the supermarket and he offers to sell her his car for £3,000. Sandra asks whether he might consider a slightly lower price. Mohammed shakes his head and then says that the offer is open until 5pm on Friday. Sandra is unsure of whether Mohammed lives at number 34 or 56 Shakespeare Drive and decides to send a letter accepting his offer to number 34. Sandra doesn't watch the news and is unaware that there is a seven-day postal strike starting the next day. Sandra posts the letter on Monday at 4pm. Mohammed changes his mind and decides to telephone Sandra informing her of this fact. He leaves a message on her answerphone at 4.05pm on that Monday. Sandra never checks her answerphone. On Thursday, Sandra bumps into Mohammed at the chemist and informs him, 'I've accepted your offer'; however, Mohammed is listening to his MP3 player and does not hear her.

Advise Sandra as to whether there is a binding contract between her and Mohammed.

Unilateral offers

Where the offeror makes a unilateral offer to the world, acceptance takes place on performance of the act required under the terms of the offer. There is no need for the offeree to notify the offeror of his acceptance of the unilateral offer. An example of this is *Carlill* in which acceptance was deemed to take place upon performance of an act, namely using the smoke ball and catching influenza.

SUMMARY

- The key difference between an invitation to treat and an offer is that an offer demonstrates a clear intention to be bound by the terms of the offer, whereas an invitation to treat is merely a demonstration of a willingness to negotiate terms.
- In order for there to be a contract there must be an agreement between the parties. This requires an unambiguous offer that is communicated to the offeree, and an acceptance that unequivocally mirrors the terms of the offer, and is communicated to the offeror prior to any revocation of the offer.
- Acceptance of an offer must generally be communicated to the offeror, but there are two exceptions to this rule; namely where the postal rule applies and where there is a unilateral offer.

FURTHER READING

Beatson J, Burrows A and Cartwright J, *Anson's Law of Contract*, 29th edn (Oxford University Press, 2010) – Refer to this textbook for an advanced look at the issues discussed in this chapter.

Capps D, 'Electronic mail and the postal rule' (2004) 15(7) ICCLR 207 – This article examines the effect of modern-day communication methods on the postal rule.

Gardner S, 'Trashing with Trollope: A deconstruction of the postal rules in contract' (1992) 12 Oxford Journal of Legal Studies 170 – considers how the postal service in the nineteenth century gave rise to the postal rule.

Stone R, *The Modern Law of Contract*, 9th edn (Routledge, 2011) – Refer to this textbook for a more advanced exploration of the issues raised in this chapter.

Stone R, *Q&A Contract Law 2012–2013* (Routledge, 2012) – This book will help you to prepare for your exams.

Unger J, 'Self-service shops and the law of contract' (1953) 16 MLR 369 – This article provides an analysis of the decision in *Pharmaceutical Society of Great Britain v Boots Cash Chemists (Southern) Ltd* and consideration of the operation of the rules of offer and acceptance in self-service shops.

Winfield PH, 'Some aspects of offer and acceptance' (1939) 55 LQR 499 – This article provides an early consideration of the rules relating to offer and acceptance and remains influential to this day.

COMPANION WEBSITE

An online glossary compiled by the authors is available on the companion website: www.routledge.com/cw/beginningthelaw

Chapter 3
Elements of a contract II

LEARNING OUTCOMES

After reading this chapter, you should be able to:

- Understand what is meant by consideration
- Explain why past consideration is not good consideration
- Distinguish between promises to pay more and promises to accept less
- Consider the importance of promissory estoppel
- Understand the requirements of intention to create legal relations and capacity

INTRODUCTION

This chapter will explore the remaining three elements that are needed in order to have a valid contract. These are consideration, the intention to create legal relations and capacity. As with agreement, these elements are essential – without them, there would be no contract. Any rights and obligations that a party has would be unenforceable.

English law requires that the party enforcing a promise has provided consideration; we will look at what is meant by consideration. By contrast, in Scotland there is no requirement that consideration has been provided. The requirements of consideration have proved problematic, especially where there has been a promise to pay more or accept less. Traditionally, the party seeking to enforce the promise was unsuccessful. To find solutions to these problems we will look at the development of practical benefit and the doctrine of promissory estoppel.

The law also requires the contracting parties to intend to enter into a legal relationship; without such intention, the agreement is not enforceable. Finally, we will look at the requirement that the parties have the capacity to contract.

DEFINING CONSIDERATION

Where a person (the promisor) promises to do something for another party (the promisee), the promisee must provide something of value in the eyes of the law (known as 'consideration') in return for that promise, otherwise the promise cannot be enforced.

For example, if Roger promises (i.e. agrees) to sell a copy of *Beginning Contract Law* to Sheila, Sheila provides consideration for that promise by agreeing to pay or actually making payment. Thus, Sheila can enforce Roger's promise to sell the book to her. Equally, Roger can enforce Sheila's promise to make the payment as he has provided consideration for her promise by agreeing to sell her the book.

There are two classic definitions of consideration. One definition often quoted is found in *Dunlop Pneumatic Tyre Co Ltd v Selfridge & Co Ltd* [1915] AC 847. In this case, Lord Dunedin cited Sir Frederick Pollock's classic definition: 'An act or forbearance of one party, or the promise thereof, is the price for which the promise of the other is bought, and the promise thus given for value is enforceable.' (Pollock, *Principles of Contract*, 8th edn, p175).

The other classic definition was given by Lush J in the case of *Currie v Misa* (1875) LR 10 Ex 153: 'A valuable consideration, in the sense of the law, may consist either in some right, interest, profit, or benefit accruing to the one party, or some forbearance, detriment, loss, or responsibility, given, suffered, or undertaken by the other.' (at p162).

This definition demonstrates that consideration is based upon either the promisor receiving a benefit, or the promisee suffering a detriment at the request of the promisor. For example, if Marie promises to give Mick £100 in exchange for Mick mending her fence, the consideration provided by Mick is a detriment to him, but is also a benefit to Marie. As Lush J states, consideration must be 'a valuable consideration' in the eyes of the law. Consideration is not limited to money and tangible objects, but can cover situations where the promisee performs an act to his detriment. In the section headed 'Principles of consideration' below, we will explore the rules relating to what can and what cannot amount to consideration.

Students often find the concept of consideration a difficult one to grasp. However, a handy tip is to begin by identifying the promises that have been made in any given scenario, and then look for what has been given in exchange for that promise (this is the consideration). The general rule is that if there is no consideration given in exchange for the promise, then the promise is unenforceable. However, there are some exceptions to this general rule, which will be explored below.

Key Definitions

Promisor – The person making the promise.
Promisee – The person who will attempt to enforce the promise.

PRINCIPLES OF CONSIDERATION

There are a number of general principles that underpin the law on consideration. These will be explained below.

Consideration must be sufficient

'Consideration must be sufficient' means that the consideration provided must be something of value in the eyes of the law. In *White v Bluett* (1853) 23 LJ Ex 36, the father was owed a sum of money by his son. The son was continually berating his father about how he managed his affairs. In order to silence his son, the father offered to write off the debt if the son would stop berating him. The court later held that the son could not enforce his father's promise because his ceasing to berate his father was not something of value in the eyes of the law: in other words, it was not good consideration. Why? This was because the father had received nothing tangible in return for his promise.

In *Hamer v Sidway* (1891) 27 NE 256 (an American case), an uncle promised his nephew a sum of money if he abstained from a number of vices – drinking, gambling and smoking – until his 21st birthday. The New York courts held this to be good consideration and the nephew could enforce his uncle's promise. Unlike in *White v Bluett* the nephew had a right to do these things and therefore he had provided something tangible, as there was forbearance on his part. This is interesting because if you give up something that you have a right to do, this can amount to good consideration in the eyes of the law. Had the uncle promised the nephew a sum of money just because of his natural love and affection, this would have been unenforceable by the nephew as this is an intangible return and would not be of value in the eyes of the law.

On-the-spot question

? Sarah, who is 17 years old, smokes 80 cigarettes a day. Her father William is concerned about her health and promises to buy her a horse if she stops smoking. Her mother Hillary loves her very much and on a separate occasion tells her that she will give her £12,000 next year, saying 'nothing makes a parent happier than making sure that their children are well looked after'.

What would happen if William and Hillary refused to honour their promises?

Consideration need not be adequate

Although consideration must be sufficient, it need not be adequate. This means that the value of the consideration need not be of equivalent value to the promise it is given in exchange for. For example, imagine that Ferrari offered to sell you a Formula One racing car for £500. The car itself is worth £1,000,000; nevertheless, you will provide good consideration for the car by paying £500 for it because £500 is money, which clearly has some value in the eyes of the law. Thus, this is sufficient consideration (indeed £1 would be sufficient here). The fact that the true value of the car is much higher is not relevant because consideration need not be adequate (or of equivalent value). An example of this can be seen in *Chappell & Co Ltd v Nestlé Co Ltd* [1960] AC 87.

KEY CASE ANALYSIS: *Chappell & Co Ltd v Nestlé Co Ltd* **[1960] AC 87**

Background

In this case Nestlé had a customer promotion in which it advertised that customers could purchase records for 1s 6d, if they also sent in three chocolate wrappers. The claimant, Chappell, sought to prevent Nestlé selling the records, arguing that what Nestlé was doing breached the Copyright Act 1956 because the promotion amounted to a retail sale. One of the questions that the House of Lords had to decide was whether the chocolate wrappers could amount to consideration, as this would affect whether the claimants were owed royalties.

Principle established

The House of Lords held that the chocolate wrappers amounted to consideration. Giving judgment, Lord Somervell held that the wrappers were part of the consideration (given in return for the records), and stated that it was irrelevant that chocolate wrappers are considered worthless by Nestlé. Crucially, Nestlé had asked for chocolate wrappers and the customer, by giving Nestlé what they wanted, had provided sufficient consideration. It is clear that consideration need not be adequate. As Lord Somervell states:

> A contracting party can stipulate for what consideration he chooses. A peppercorn does not cease to be good consideration if it is established that the promisee does not like pepper and will throw away the corn.

Consideration must move from the promisee

In *Thomas v Thomas* (1842) 2 QB 851, the court dealt with a case concerning a widow who had been promised property by her husband. The court held that a pious wish by the testator to look after his wife was not good consideration, since according to Patteson J, 'Motive is not the same thing with consideration . . . legally speaking, it forms no part of the consideration'. What was consideration was the ground rent payable by the widow. Crucially, Patteson J said that consideration in 'all events . . . must be moving from the plaintiff'. For example, this means that if Louise and Danielle enter into an agreement that Louise will give Danielle £50 as soon as June gives Louise £75, then Danielle could not enforce the promise since she has not provided any consideration. The consideration for the £75 is being provided by June, therefore the consideration does not move from the promisee.

Rule against past consideration

There is a further rule that past consideration is not good consideration. This is best explained by way of an example: on Monday, Robert paints Kim's house as a surprise. On Wednesday, Kim returns home and is very happy. On Thursday, Kim promises Robert £100 as a thank-you present; however, Kim never gives Robert the £100. Here Robert would argue that, as the promisee, he should be able to enforce Kim's promise. Robert would argue that painting the house is sufficient consideration (i.e. something of value in the eyes of law); however, it is past consideration because Robert painted the house prior to Kim's promise, and therefore it is not good consideration. He has not supported Kim's promise with new consideration. If Kim had instead said, 'Thank you, if you paint the door you have missed I will give you £100 as a present', then Robert would provide fresh consideration to support the promise. In *Eastwood v Kenyon* (1840) 113 ER 482, the guardian of a girl borrowed money to finance her upbringing and education. When the girl got married, her new husband promised to reimburse the guardian for his expenses. The promise was unenforceable because the expenditure happened before the promise and was therefore past consideration. Lord Denman CJ stated that there could be no enforcement as there was 'no consideration but a past benefit not conferred at the request of the defendant'. There is an exception to the common law rule known as implied assumpsit. This exception was not found to be present in *Eastwood v Kenyon*.

The key case for implied assumpsit is *Lampleigh v Braithwaite* (1615) Hobart 105. Here the promisor was due to be executed and begged his friend (the promisee) to ask the king for a pardon. The pardon was granted and the promisor promised £1,000 to the promisee but then refused to honour the promise. The court held that the promise was enforceable because there would have been an implied understanding that the requested act would be rewarded, therefore the later promise was held to be enforceable as the act performed had been in expectation of that promise. In *Re Casey's Patents* [1892] 1 Ch 104, the Court of

Appeal held that an act performed prior to the promisor's promise might amount to consideration if, according to Bowen LJ, there was 'an implication that at the time it was rendered it was to be paid for, and . . . when you get in the subsequent document a promise to pay, that promise may be treated . . . as an admission which evidences . . . the amount of that reasonable remuneration on the faith of which the service was originally rendered'. The modern test for implied assumpsit comes from *Pao On v Lau Yiu Long* [1980] AC 165.

KEY CASE ANALYSIS: *Pao On v Lau Yiu Long* **[1980] AC 614**

Background

This case involved the sale of shares by the claimant to the defendant. Due to the complex business arrangements involved, the defendants had agreed to indemnify the claimants against the possible fall in the price of the shares. One of the questions that the Privy Council had to consider was whether an act done by the promisee at the promisor's request in the past could amount to consideration to enforce their agreement.

Principle established

The Privy Council held that the requested act could amount to consideration, notwithstanding that it was done before the parties' final agreement. Implied assumpsit was used as an exception to the rule against past consideration. Lord Scarman established the requirements needed for implied assumpsit to be relied upon:

1. The act must have been at the promisor's request,
2. The parties must have understood that the act would be remunerated, and
3. Payment would have been legally enforceable had it been promised in advance.

Existing duties

Where there is an existing legal duty to perform the requested act, then performing that act cannot amount to consideration. In *Collins v Godefroy* (1831) 1 B & A 950, a person had agreed to give evidence at court, in return for which he would be paid. However, he was subpoenaed and this meant that he was under a legal obligation to give evidence, which in turn meant that he could not enforce the promise as he had not provided consideration. Equally, a police officer who is offered £500 to catch a thief by the victim of a theft could not enforce that promise if they caught the thief.

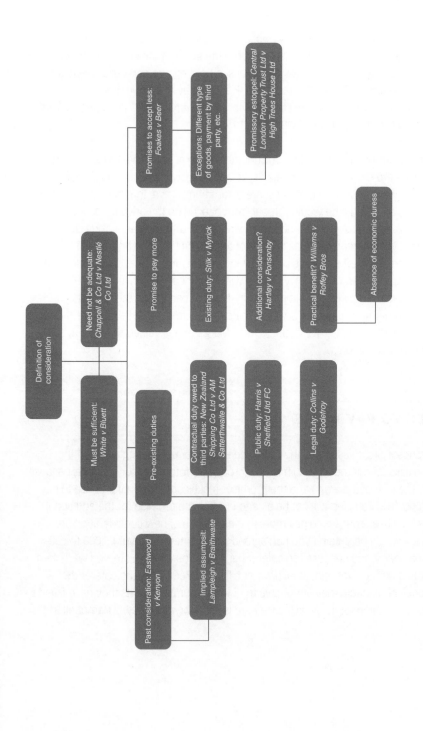

There are good public policy reasons why public officials who have an existing public duty to carry out their job cannot enforce payments from the public. If the police are asked to go beyond their public duty, such as to provide increased policing at a particular event, then a promise by the organisers of that event to pay the police may amount to good consideration (see *Glasbrook Brothers Ltd v Glamorgan County Council* [1925] AC 270 and *Harris v Sheffield United FC Ltd* [1988] QB 77).

We have seen how forbearance can be consideration. If the act of forbearance requested is already owed as a pre-existing contractual duty to a third party, then can this amount to consideration? For example, Tom and Karl share a communal drive. Tom has family visiting next week and he asks Karl if he would forbear from parking on the drive for a week. In return, Tom promises Karl £200. If Karl does not park on the drive he can enforce Tom's promise? If Tom's wife Margaret also asks Karl not to park on the drive and promises him £100, can Karl then enforce Margaret's promise? Karl has incurred no additional detriment as he has already promised a third party that he will not park on the drive. Despite a pre-existing contractual duty owed to a third party, Karl not parking on the drive might provide good consideration: see *New Zealand Shipping Co Ltd v AM Satterthwaite & Co Ltd, The Eurymedon* [1975] AC 154, Privy Council. Thus, Margaret has gained the right to sue Karl should he park on the drive.

PROMISES TO PAY MORE

Where the promisor promises to pay the promisee £5,000 for performing an act, if the promisee then asks for another £1,000 midway through performance (for instance, because he misquoted the cost of the work) and the promisor makes an additional promise to pay that extra £1,000, the promisee will not be able to enforce the promise for the additional £1,000. This is because promises to pay more in the absence of new consideration are unenforceable. It would be unfair if you had agreed with a caterer a fee of £3,000 to cater for your birthday party, and because the caterer has given you a low quote, you were then confronted with a demand for additional payment. If you agree to pay the caterer the additional money demanded, they are unable to enforce your promise as they have failed to provide any consideration for it. The key case here is *Stilk v Myrick* (1809) 2 Campbell 317.

KEY CASE ANALYSIS: *Stilk v Myrick* (1809) 2 Campbell 317

Background

This case involved sailors who were serving on a ship in the Baltic Sea. Several members of the crew had deserted and the captain had subsequently agreed to divide their wages amongst the remaining crew members. Afterwards, the captain broke his promise and the sailors sued him for the additional payment. Garrow, for the defendant, had argued that their claim should be defeated on grounds of public policy, since it was not unusual for many sailors to die or desert, and allowing the sailors to recover the additional money would invite future claims (i.e. there might be a risk of duress). The issue was whether the sailors could enforce the captain's promise to pay more.

Principle established

The court held that the sailors had provided no consideration for the additional payment and therefore the captain's promise to pay was not enforceable.

Lord Ellenborough stated that the sailors had done nothing additional to their original contractual obligations and therefore:

> those who remain are bound by the terms of their original contract to exert themselves to the utmost to bring the ship in safety to her destined port. Therefore, without looking to the policy of this agreement, I think it is void for want of consideration . . .

Lord Ellenborough took the view that if the facts had been different and the sailors had left as a result of the captain's actions (i.e. if the sailors had been dismissed, rather than deserted), then the act of the remaining sailors in completing the voyage would have amounted to new consideration. However, *Stilk* is a confusing case, as Espinasse's law report [*Stilk v Myrick* (1809) 6 Espinasse 129] stated that Lord Ellenborough's decision was based on preventing **duress** (i.e. the fact that the captain might have been coerced).

In *Hartley v Ponsonby* (1857) 7 Ellis and Blackburn 872, a captain of a ship agreed to pay the sailors additional money if they continued with their voyage after a large number of sailors deserted the ship. This case can be distinguished from *Stilk* because (i) so many of the crew deserted that it was unsafe to continue the voyage, and therefore the sailors were discharged from performing the rest of the voyage, and (ii) the extra payment was in the best interests of the ship owner and there was no duress. By agreeing to continue the voyage, the sailors had provided fresh consideration to enforce the additional payment. Similarly, in *Hanson v Royden* (1867–68) LR 3 CP 47, a sailor was promoted to second mate and was promised an increased salary. This promise was enforceable because the sailor had gone beyond what was required by his original promise by performing the duties of the second mate.

KEY CASE ANALYSIS: *Williams v Roffey Bros & Nicholls (Contractors) Ltd* [1990] 2 WLR 1153

Background

In this case a carpentry firm had agreed to help refurbish 27 flats. Midway through the work the carpentry firm fell into financial difficulties as they had failed to realise the actual cost of carrying out the work (their quote had been too low at £20,000). The defendants promised to pay an additional £10,300 as they needed to have the building project completed on time or risk paying a penalty for late completion. The issue was whether a promise to pay more could be enforceable, despite the carpentry firm not providing additional consideration in return for the extra payment.

Principle established

Controversially, the Court of Appeal allowed a claim for additional money for performance of an existing duty to succeed where the promisee had provided no additional consideration in the traditional sense. The Court of Appeal held that if the promisee had provided the promisor with a 'practical benefit' by continuing with their work in return for the additional payment, then that practical benefit could amount to consideration.

Glidewell LJ stated that:

(i)   if A has entered into a contract with B to do work for, or to supply goods or services to, B in return for payment by B; and

(ii) at some stage before A has completely performed his obligations under the contract, B has reason to doubt whether A will, or will be able to, complete his side of the bargain; and

(iii) B thereupon promises A an additional payment in return for A's promise to perform his contractual obligations on time; and

(iv) as a result of giving his promise, B obtains in practice a benefit, or obviates a disbenefit; and

(v)   B's promise is not given as a result of economic duress or fraud on the part of A; then

(vi) the benefit to B is capable of being consideration for B's promise, so that the promise will be legally binding.

Williams v Roffey Bros & Nicholls (Contractors) Ltd [1990] 2 WLR 1153 is an extremely important case because it permits the enforceability of a promise to pay more where no additional consideration has been given. On the facts, the carpentry firm had provided the defendants with a practical benefit by:

- the carpenters being able to continue working for them,
- as they did not delay the work, the defendant would not be liable for a penalty for delay, and
- the defendants were saved the trouble for looking for new carpenters.

Glidewell LJ considered the decision in *Stilk v Myrick* and stated that this remained good law where the promisor 'secures no benefit by his promise'. This means that if there is a practical benefit in the absence of economic duress, then a promise to pay more will be enforceable by the promisee. If there is not a practical benefit, then *Stilk v Myrick* shall apply and the promise to pay more will not be enforceable.

On-the-spot question

Flyaway Airlines employ Michael and Stuart as cabin crew. To operate safely, each flight requires at least four members of cabin crew. One of the cabin crew turns up to work drunk and is unable to work. Along with Michael and Stuart there are two other members of cabin crew on the flight. After a disagreement before take-off, the airline promises Michael and Stuart an extra £250 bonus each as the airline believes that they will have to work a lot harder to serve all the customers and to avoid any complaints.

Can Michael and Stuart enforce the promise for an additional £250 each?

PROMISES TO ACCEPT LESS

A promise to accept less in discharge of a debt is not good consideration. This means that where the promisor is owed £1,000 by the promisee, if they promise the promisee that they will accept £700 in settlement of the debt, that promise is unenforceable. Consequently, the promisor is entitled to recover an additional £300. In *Pinnel's Case* (1602) 5 Rep 117a, Sir Edward Coke stated that a promise to pay less was not enforceable, but that there could be exceptions that would be capable of discharging the remaining debt. These exceptions could include accepting payment earlier than it was due, or at a different place, or by accepting something in addition to the requested payment (such as a cloak or a hawk). The decision in *Pinnel's Case* was reconfirmed by the House of Lords in *Foakes v Beer* (1884) 9 App Cas 605.

KEY CASE ANALYSIS: *Foakes v Beer* (1884) 9 App Cas 605

Background

In this case a sum of over £2,000 was owed. It was agreed that the debtor would pay the sum in instalments and would then not have to pay any interest owed. However, the creditor subsequently demanded the interest owed under the contract. The issue was whether a promise to accept less was enforceable.

Principle established

The House of Lords held that the promise to pay less was not enforceable and that the interest was still payable. Lord Blackburn dissented, as His Lordship believed, 'that all men of business, whether merchants or tradesmen, do every day recognise and act on the ground that prompt payment of a part of their demand may be more beneficial to them than it would be to insist on their rights and enforce payment of the whole'. Applying Lord Blackburn's reasoning, this means that prompt payment by a debtor could amount to good consideration to enforce the promise to accept less. It is important to note that this was not the opinion of the majority. The majority were reluctant to depart from the rule in *Pinnel's Case* that there was no good consideration for a promise to accept less in discharge of a debt.

It is clear that if there is some benefit such as something in addition or as an alternative to the debt, or if the debt is paid at an earlier date or at a different place, then this can amount to consideration.

Could a 'practical benefit' apply to promises to accept less? Lord Blackburn identified that there could be a practical benefit in accepting less in return for prompt repayment. In *Re*

Selectmove Ltd [1995] 1 WLR 474, Peter Gibson LJ rejected extending the decision of *Williams v Roffey Bros*. In this case, taxes were owed to the Inland Revenue and a tax inspector had arranged that the tax owed could be paid by instalments. The Inland Revenue demanded payment in full. The Court of Appeal held that the company had provided no consideration to enforce the promise. In *Re Selectmove Ltd* the Court of Appeal rejected the argument that a practical benefit could amount to consideration. Peter Gibson LJ stated that:

> When a creditor and a debtor . . . reach agreement on the payment of the debt by instalments to accommodate the debtor, the creditor will no doubt always see a practical benefit to himself in so doing . . . that was a matter expressly considered in *Foakes v Beer* yet held not to constitute good consideration in law. *Foakes v Beer* was not even referred to in *Williams v Roffey Bros & Nicholls (Contractors) Ltd* [1991] 1 QB 1, and it is in my judgment impossible, consistently with the doctrine of precedent, for this court to extend the principle of Williams's case to any circumstances governed by the principle of *Foakes v Beer* . . .

Therefore, we can see that the person enforcing the promise to accept less will not be able to rely upon the fact that they have provided the promisor with a practical benefit to enforce their promise.

PROMISSORY ESTOPPEL

The equitable doctrine of promissory estoppel is a further exception to the rule that promises to accept less in discharge of a debt will not amount to good consideration. Promissory estoppel is where equity assists the promisee. The key case is *Central London Property Trust Ltd v High Trees House Ltd* [1947] KB 130.

KEY CASE ANALYSIS: *Central London Property Trust Ltd v High Trees House Ltd* [1947] KB 130

Background

In this case a building was half let to tenants because of the Second World War. It was agreed that the owners of the building would accept reduced rent of £1,250 while the building was not fully let. After the war had finished, the full rent was demanded as the building was now fully let.

Principles established

Denning J revived the doctrine of promissory estoppel to protect a party who had relied on a promise to accept less and who was subsequently faced with a demand for payment in full by the promisor. Denning J held that this promise was protected by promissory estoppel and that the owners would have been prevented from demanding the remaining rent before the building was fully occupied. However, the promise was not valid for the period when the building was fully occupied. This meant that full rent was payable for the last two-quarters of 1945.

Importantly, the case was not argued on estoppel as all that was being claimed was the last two-quarters of rent. However, Denning J stated that the period protected by the promise could 'cease when the conditions to which the representation applied came to an end, or it also might be said that it would only come to an end on notice. In either case it is only a way of ascertaining the scope of the representation'.

In *Combe v Combe* [1951] 2 KB 215 the Court of Appeal stated that promissory estoppel could not be used as a sword (i.e. as a cause of action). It was only a shield (i.e. used only as a defence). The case concerned an action by a divorced wife seeking to enforce the promise of payment by her former husband, which was found to be unenforceable for lack of consideration. Denning LJ reiterated the requirements of promissory estoppel:

- There needs to be, by words or conduct, a promise made that was intended to affect the parties' legal relations – i.e. a promise to waive the contractual obligations.
- The promise needs to be acted upon – i.e. cease paying the money due.
- During the period that the qualifications to the promise remain (i.e. reduced rent while you are looking for work), the promisor cannot go back on their word and enforce their legal rights.

As Denning J had stated in *High Trees*, it is important to understand what had been originally meant by the representation. Crucially, it must be inequitable to go back on your promise. An example of when it would not be inequitable to go back on your promise is the case of *D&C Builders Ltd v Rees* [1966] 2 QB 617. Here, Lord Denning MR permitted builders to recover the full amount of the money owed by their clients. This was because the clients had fully understood the builders' financial difficulties and had forced them to accept a lesser amount.

But what about the original amount that has been waived? In *High Trees* the claimants had not sought to recover the waived rent. Promissory estoppel suspends the right to full payment whilst the conditions exist (i.e. in this case, during the war) with the right of recovering full rent being revived by the expiry of these conditions. However, it would appear that promissory estoppel can also extinguish the right to recover the waived rent during the period that these conditions exist. This would appear to suggest that whilst being suspensory in relation to ongoing obligations, promissory estoppel can extinguish the debt or any other periodic payment during this period.

In *Tool Metal Manufacturing Co Ltd v Tungsten Electric Co Ltd* [1955] 1 WLR 761, the royalty payments that were waived during the Second World War could be recovered after a notice seeking full payment was served. Only then could the promisor start to demand the payment of royalties from the date given. Promissory estoppel merely suspended the obligation to make payments owed for the duration of the war (the promisor could ask for payments to recommence once the war was over), but there was no right to recover the waived payments (these were extinguished).

On-the-spot question

 Does the doctrine of promissory estoppel extinguish or suspend the promisor's rights to recover the money owed?

Discuss.

INTENTION TO CREATE LEGAL RELATIONS

The courts presume that where an agreement is made in a family and social situation, the parties did not intend to contract; hence their agreement will be unenforceable. Conversely, where an agreement is made in a commercial setting, the courts will presume that the parties intended to contract. The key case for domestic and social agreements is *Balfour v Balfour* [1919] 2 KB 571.

KEY CASE ANALYSIS: *Balfour v Balfour* [1919] 2 KB 571

Background

A husband and wife had entered into an agreement that stated that the husband would pay the wife a sum of money. The husband did not honour the agreement. The wife sued for breach of contract. The issue was whether there was a binding contract between the parties. Crucial to this was whether there had been an intention to create legal relations.

Principle established

The Court of Appeal held that where husbands and wives enter into an agreement, they are deemed by the courts not to have entered into a contract. This is because the courts presume that they do not have the intention to enter into legal relations. Therefore, the husband's promise was unenforceable.

Atkin LJ was not in favour of enforcing such agreements: 'To my mind it would be of the worst possible example to hold that agreements such as this resulted in legal obligations which could be enforced in the Courts.'

This presumption is a rebuttable one. This means that a party to an agreement can submit evidence to the court that they actually intended to create legal relations.

Parties to a business agreement are presumed to have intended to create legal relations. However, there are examples of when one of the parties has successfully argued that they did not intend to create legal relations. In *Rose and Frank v Compton Ltd* [1925] AC 445, the presumption was rebutted because the contract contained an honour clause, which stated the parties would resolve any disagreements without going to court. The effect of the parties not having the intention to create legal relations is that there is no contract and no recourse to the courts to resolve disputes.

CAPACITY TO CONTRACT

In order for there to be a valid contract, the parties must have capacity to contract. If a party does not have capacity then the contract shall be unenforceable. Minors (children) under the age of 18 do not have the capacity to enter into contracts. An exception to this is a contract for necessaries, which includes food, housing, clothing, training and education. In *Nash v Inman* [1908] 2 KB 1, a student purchased waistcoats from a tailor. However, the student later refused to pay for the waistcoats. The tailor's claim for breach of contract failed because this was not a contract of necessaries because the student had no need of the waistcoats. In *Proform Sports Management Ltd v Proactive Sports Management Ltd* [2006] EWHC 2903, a football managing company sued Wayne Rooney for breaching their contract, when he entered into another contract with a third party. The court ruled that Mr Rooney was not liable for breach of contract because he was a minor when he entered into the contract, and therefore he lacked capacity. This meant that the contract was **voidable** and unenforceable against Rooney, because the contract was not one of necessaries.

People who lack mental capacity or who are drunk when they enter into a contract also lack capacity to contract (i.e. the contract is voidable). A company has a separate legal personality, which means that it is distinct from those who run and own the company. The company's capacity to contract can be limited in its memorandum of association.

SUMMARY

- For an agreement to be enforceable, sufficient consideration must move from the promisee. Consideration need not be adequate and past consideration is generally not good consideration.
- Performance of an existing duty does not constitute consideration for a promise to pay more, unless new consideration is provided or the promisor receives practical benefit. A promise to accept less is generally not good consideration for part payment of a debt, although there are exceptions to this rule, including promissory estoppel.
- The parties must intend to create legal relations and have the capacity to contract.

READING LIST

Beatson J, Burrows A and Cartwright J, *Anson's Law of Contract*, 29th edn (Oxford University Press, 2010) – Refer to this textbook for an advanced look at the issues discussed in this chapter.

Blair A and Hird NJ, 'Minding your own business – *Williams v Roffey* re-visited: consideration re-considered' [1996] JBL 254 – This article reconsiders the law on consideration in some detail.

Halson R, 'Case Comment: Sailors, sub-contractors and consideration' [1990] LQR 183 – This is an interesting case commentary of *Williams v Roffey Bros*.

Stone R, *The Modern Law of Contract*, 9th edn (Routledge, 2011) – Refer to this textbook for a more advanced exploration of the issues raised in this chapter.

Stone R, *Q&A Contract Law 2012–2013* (Routledge, 2012) – This book will help you to prepare for your exams.

COMPANION WEBSITE

An online glossary compiled by the authors is available on the companion website: www.routledge.com/cw/beginningthelaw

Chapter 4
Terms of a contract and exemption clauses

LEARNING OUTCOMES

After reading this chapter, you should be able to:

- Understand the difference between a term and a representation
- Distinguish between express and implied terms
- Explain the effects of breaching a condition, warranty and innominate term
- Describe the ways in which a term is incorporated into a contract
- Consider the construction of an exemption clause
- Understand the effect of UCTA 1977 and the UTCCR 1999

INTRODUCTION

We all enter into contracts every day. For example, when you buy a coffee from a shop you enter into a contract, even though there is no paperwork; however, this is an oral contract and, as we shall see, this contract contains terms. This may surprise you since we think of terms as being written down on a formal contractual document, but there are in fact many terms in such a straightforward transaction:

- There are **express terms** that you have expressly agreed with the seller. This would include the price and the type of coffee you have ordered.
- There are **implied terms** that are implied by law into your contract, such as that the coffee is of satisfactory quality.
- But what about a statement made by the seller during pre-contractual negotiations which induces the other party to enter into the contract but is not intended to become part of the contract (e.g., 'This coffee contains fewer than 100 calories')? This is likely to be a representation. If this is false, you can sue the seller for **misrepresentation**.
- How about the statement: 'This is the smoothest coffee in the world'? This is **mere puff** and not a term of the contract. If this is false, you will not be able to sue the seller.

On-the-spot question

Can you think of any other contracts that you have entered into recently? Consider what the terms of the contract were.

This chapter provides an overview of the contents of a contract. We will distinguish between a term (which is so important to the parties that they intended it to become part of the contract) and a representation (which is a statement that induces a party to enter into a contract). This is important if, at a later stage, the representation turns out to be false or the term is not complied with. You will need to be able to determine whether you are dealing with a term or a representation in order to advise the innocent party as to their rights.

DISTINGUISHING TERMS AND REPRESENTATIONS

Prior to contracting and during negotiations, parties to a contract will make a number of statements to one another. Some of these statements will be included in the contract as terms, whereas others will not be part of the contract but will be known as representations. Other statements may be classified as mere puffs. These are not statements of fact but are mere advertising puffs (or 'sales talk'), which are ambiguous and cannot be sued upon if found to be false. A famous example is 'Probably the best lager in the world'. Can you think of any other examples of mere puffs?

Distinguishing between terms and representations is important should the statement turn out to be incorrect or if it is not complied with. Where the statement is deemed to be a term of the contract, the innocent party's remedy would lie in an action for breach of contract. The innocent party may be entitled to claim **damages** or to repudiate the contract (**repudiation**), meaning that the parties' obligations under the contract are brought to an end. By contrast, where the statement is deemed to be a representation, the innocent party's remedy would lie in an action for misrepresentation. Here, the innocent party may be able to claim damages and rescind the contract (**rescission**), meaning that the parties' obligations under the contract will be set aside and they will be returned to their original positions.

The main test used to determine whether a statement is a term or a representation is based upon whether the parties intended that the statement be one which, if false, would entitle the innocent party to repudiate the contract: *Heilbut, Symons & Co v Buckleton* [1913] AC 30. In determining whether the parties intended the statement to amount to a

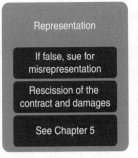

term of the contract, a number of factors are considered, such as the importance of the statement to the parties, whether either party had any special skill or knowledge, whether the parties had taken steps to verify the truth of the statement, the timing of the statement and whether the statement was included in the written contract.

Importance of the statement

Where one party makes a statement to the other party and makes it clear that a particular matter is of importance to him in contracting, then the statement is more likely to be interpreted as a term of the contract. An example of this can be seen in *Bannerman v White* (1861) 10 CB NS 844.

KEY CASE ANALYSIS: *Bannerman v White* **(1861) 10 CB NS 844**

Background

The defendant was purchasing hops from the claimant and asked the claimant whether the hops had been treated with sulphur. The claimant responded, 'No'. The defendant made it clear that he would not buy the hops should sulphur have been used because he would not have been able to sell the hops on. The issue in this case was whether the statement that the hops had not been treated was a term or a representation.

Principle established

The court held that the statement was a term since it was clearly of importance to the defendant and the claimant knew this. Thus, the importance of the statement was a factor in determining whether a statement was a term or representation.

Special skill or knowledge

Where the maker of the statement has no special skill or knowledge in the matter stated, but the other party does have such expertise, the statement is more likely to be a representation than a term. For example, in the case of *Oscar Chess Ltd v Williams* [1953] 1 WLR 370, the defendant sold a car to the claimant company on the basis that it was a 1948 model. The defendant's description of the car was based upon the date in the registration book. It later transpired that the car was a 1939 model and the claimant sought to recover damages from the defendant for breach of a term of sale. The Court of Appeal held that as the defendant had no special knowledge or skill on the matter and the claimant company were in fact car dealers, the statement as to the age of the car was not a term but a representation. However, where the maker of the statement does have expertise in the matter, the statement is more likely to be a term of the contract as in *Dick Bentley Productions Ltd v Harold Smith (Motors) Ltd* [1965] 1 WLR 623. In this case, the claimant bought a car from the defendant car dealers. The defendant made a statement to the effect that the car had only done 20,000 miles. This later transpired to be false and the car had in fact done around 100,000 miles. The claimant brought an action against the defendant company on the basis that the description of the mileage was a term of the contract. The Court of Appeal held that the statement as to the mileage constituted a term because the defendant car dealers had special skill or expertise and should have known better than to rely on the reading on the milometer.

On-the-spot question

 Why did the courts decide the cases of *Oscar Chess* and *Dick Bentley* differently?

Verification

Where the maker of the statement assures the other party that he can rely upon the statement and does not need to verify the truth of it, the statement is more likely to be treated as a term of the contract – see for example *Schawel v Reade* [1913] 2 IR 81.

EXPRESS TERMS

As stated above, a contract can be made orally and in writing. The parties will make statements during contractual negotiations and these, if regarded as terms, will be what the parties expressly agreed to be bound by. Therefore, the parties in a written contract will expressly state their contractual obligations. For instance, the buyer will expressly state that she will pay for the goods on a certain date and the seller will expressly state when the goods will be delivered. We will look at how terms are incorporated into a contract in the section headed 'Incorporation of terms into a contract' below.

In the absence of express terms such as price, terms might be implied into the contract by law. We will look at implied terms in the next section. Conversely, parties are often able to expressly state what will happen and restrict the application of implied terms. This is relevant where the implied term offers one of the parties protection and we will look at **exclusion clauses** and limitation clauses below.

Parties might argue that the express terms in a written contract might not be the totality of what they had agreed. One party might try to argue that there were further terms that had been agreed and that these were not included in the written contract. The party seeking to rely on these terms will ask that the court take these into account. English law generally excludes such extrinsic evidence; this is known as the **parol evidence rule**. However, there are exceptions to this rule, which include **collateral contracts**, contracts that were intended to be partially oral and in writing, and where there is alleged mistake, fraud or misrepresentation.

IMPLIED TERMS

Terms may be implied into a contract in one of three ways: by statute, by the courts or by custom.

Terms implied by statute

Terms may be implied into a contract by statute. Parliament has restricted the freedom of parties to contract in order to ensure that the weaker party (usually the consumer in a contract for sale or services) is protected against the party in the stronger bargaining position. We will explore the terms implied by statute into two types of contract: contracts for the sale of goods, which are governed by the Sale of Goods Act 1979 (SGA 1979); and contracts for services, which are governed by the Supply of Goods and Services Act 1982 (SGSA 1982). It is important to be able to distinguish between each type of contract in order to determine which statute will apply.

On-the-spot question

which of the following are contracts for the sale of goods and which are contracts for services?

- You travel by bus to university
- You buy a custom-made laptop
- You pay to have a portrait painted of you by a famous artist

The case of *Robinson v Graves* [1935] 1 KB 579 states that it is necessary to question what the substance of the contract was. This might be confusing as often contracts governed by the SGSA 1982 will include those where goods are supplied as part of that contract. An example of such a contract would be a builder who fits a new kitchen; this service and the quality of the kitchen cabinets and appliances would be governed by the SGSA 1982. However, if you were to purchase the appliances and cabinets yourself from a DIY store, the contract for sale, and thus the quality of the goods, would be governed by the SGA 1979.

Contracts for the sale of goods

Have you ever wondered what the phrase 'your statutory rights are not affected' means on a receipt? The SGA 1979 implies a number of terms into both business and consumer contracts for sale. Section 12(1) implies a term into the contract that the seller has title to the goods; this means that there is an implied term that the seller has the right to sell the goods. In the case of *Niblett v Confectioners' Materials Co Ltd* [1921] 3 KB 387, the court held that there had been a breach of the implied term as to title where the goods infringed another party's trademark. If the implied term under s 12(1) is breached, the buyer can demand a full refund irrespective of how long he has had the goods and whether he is able to return the goods: see *Rowland v Divall* [1923] 2 KB 500 and *Butterworth v Kingsway Motors* [1954] 1 WLR 1286.

Section 13(1) SGA 1979 implies into a contract a term that the goods sold by description will correspond to their description. Section 13 applies to both unascertained goods (goods that are not identified at time of contracting) and specific goods (goods that are identified at time of contracting). If the buyer would select the goods himself from the counter, then s 13 could still apply: *Grant v Australian Knitting Mills Ltd* [1936] AC 85 PC. Not every word will form part of the contractual description as there must be reliance upon the description provided by the seller: *Harlingdon & Leinster Enterprises Ltd v Christopher Hill Fine Art* [1991] 1 QB 564.

Section 14(2) states the goods supplied must be of satisfactory quality. This section only applies where the seller is selling in the course of a business and a one-off sale is sufficient for these purposes (*Stevenson v Rogers* [1999] QB 1028). This does not mean the goods have to be acceptable, or what the buyer herself considers to be satisfactory; rather the test is based on what the reasonable person will regard as satisfactory. Under s 14(2A), 'goods are of satisfactory quality if they meet the standard that a reasonable person would regard as satisfactory, taking account of any description of the goods, the price (if relevant) and all the other relevant circumstances'. The court also takes into account the factors listed under s 14(2B), which include fitness for the common purpose for which goods are supplied, appearance and finish, freedom from minor defects, safety and durability. The implied term under s 14(2) does not apply to defects that the buyer has made known to the seller before contracting and when the buyer took the opportunity to examine the goods and the examination ought to reveal the defect (s 14(2C)).

Section 14(3) states that the goods must be fit for the particular purpose that has been made known to the seller by the buyer. This section also only applies where the seller is selling in the course of a business. Crucially, the buyer must have relied upon the seller's skill and judgment and it must have been reasonable for him to do so.

Section 15 applies where goods are sold by sample and this section implies a term into such a contract for sale that the goods supplied will correspond to the sample in quality and 'that the goods will be free from any defect, [making their quality unsatisfactory], which would not be apparent on reasonable examination of the sample'.

On-the-spot question

?

Granny Smith has been making cakes in her kitchen to sell at the local fete for years. Her earnings enable her to go on holiday to Italy every summer. If Granny Smith was to sell her set of cake tins, do you think that she would be a seller in the course of a business?

What about Jonathan who makes his living buying and selling on internet auctions? Do you think that s 14(2) would apply to the sale of the laptop Jonathan used to buy and sell on the internet?

Contracts for services/supply of goods

In a contract for services, terms will be implied into the contract which state that the service must be carried out with reasonable care and skill (s 13, SGSA 1982), that the work will be carried out within a reasonable time if no time limit is expressly provided for in the contract (s 14(1)), and that a reasonable charge will be paid for the services if the price is not expressly stated in the contract (s 15(1)).

Terms implied by the courts

Terms may be implied into a contract by the courts in two ways: first, in certain types of contracts, such as employment contracts and landlord/tenant contracts, for example, terms will be implied into the contract by the courts. The objective here is to ensure that these types of contract are standardised and that the parties perform particular obligations in the absence of express provisions. For example, in an employment contract, the courts will imply terms such as the obligation of mutual trust and confidence between the employer and employee. This ensures that both parties are protected despite the lack of an express term to that effect. The second way in which a term may be implied into a contract by the courts is by fact. The courts are seeking to give effect to the implicit intentions of the parties. The courts will apply the 'officious bystander' test. This test questions whether the term to be implied is 'something so obvious that it goes without saying' (*Shirlaw v Southern Foundries Ltd* [1939] 2 KB 206 at 207). The court considers the response that a third party (the officious bystander) would have the question of whether the term was intended to be included in the contract. If the officious bystander would respond 'Oh, of course', then such a term will be implied into the contract. Another way in which terms may be implied into a contract by fact is through the use of the 'business efficacy' test: *The Moorcock* (1889) 14 PD 64. According to Bowen LJ, this test takes into account whether the term is necessary in order to ensure that the business transaction is effective in accordance with the intentions of the parties.

Terms implied by custom

Certain contracts relating to a specific trade or profession may have terms implied into the contract by custom or trade usage. Custom is not imposed by the courts and is not written down in statute, but it has evolved within specific trades or localities, and is what parties contracting within that trade or locality implicitly expect to occur. Any customs followed in that particular trade or locality will be incorporated into the contract implicitly so long as the custom is well known and reasonable. However, the parties are free to exclude any customs by express provision. An example of a term implied by custom is found in *Hutton v Warren* (1836) 1 M&W 466. In this case the court held that it was custom (and so a term of the contract) that the outgoing tenant of a farm was entitled to a reasonable allowance for seeds and labour to represent his investment on the land.

CLASSIFICATION OF TERMS

It is important for parties to know what their rights and liabilities will be in the event of a breach. Therefore, parties will usually attempt to classify the importance of the term at time of contracting. Depending on the classification of the term, the innocent party might have the right to repudiate the contract or just the right to claim damages.

Conditions

A condition is a term that is very important and that goes to the root of the contract. Where a condition is breached, the innocent party has the right to repudiate the contract (bring the contract to an end and be discharged from their own obligations) and claim damages for their losses.

Parties are free to classify terms as conditions. The courts will generally respect the parties' express classification; however, in *Schuler AG v Wickman Machine Tools Sales* [1974] AC 235, the House of Lords refused to treat the word 'condition' as meaning that the parties had intended there would be the right to repudiate the contract. The House reached this decision in order to avoid the innocent party being able to repudiate the contract for what was only a minor breach.

Statute will classify certain implied terms as conditions, such as ss 12–15 of the SGA 1979. If the buyer is a non-consumer and there is only a minor breach, then the implied terms under ss 13–15 SGA 1979 may be treated as warranties, which means that the buyer will not be able to repudiate the contract, but can still claim damages (s 15A).

Warranties

A warranty is a term that is not central to the contract. This was explained in *Dawsons Ltd v Bonnin* [1922] 2 AC 413 when the court stated that a warranty was 'collateral to the main purpose of . . . a contract'. If a warranty is breached, the innocent party only has the right to claim damages and may not repudiate the contract. Where the parties do not specify whether a term is to be treated as a condition or a warranty, the court will have regard to whether the term goes to the root of the contract and the effect of the breach.

Innominate terms

This is where a contract does not specify whether a term is to be classified as either a condition or a warranty. The courts will look at the effect of the actual breach upon the contract.

KEY CASE ANALYSIS: *Hong Kong Fir Shipping Co Ltd v Kawasaki Kisen Kaisha Ltd* [1962] 2 QB 26

Background

The owners of a ship agreed to deliver the ship to a charterers for hire for a specified period of time. Upon delivery of the ship, it was found to be unseaworthy. Some time after setting sail, the charterers repudiated the contract and claimed damages for breach of contract since the ship was unseaworthy. The ship owners claimed that the contract had been wrongfully repudiated. The issue that arose in this case was whether the term of seaworthiness in a contract for the charter of a ship was classified as a condition or a warranty (as this would determine whether the charterers had been entitled to repudiate the contract).

Principle established

The Court of Appeal held that the classification of the term would be decided with reference to the effect of the breach, and treated the term as an innominate term.

Upjohn LJ stated that a literal interpretation should not be given to the seaworthiness of the ship as it did not make sense to permit a party to repudiate a contract for trifling breaches, such as if a nail was missing from a timber or medical supplies were not onboard. His Lordship stated, 'It is contrary to common sense to suppose that in such circumstances the parties contemplated that the charterer should at once be entitled to treat the contract as at an end for such trifling breaches'.

However, the concept of an innominate term can be criticised as a party may believe that a term is classified as a condition and then repudiate the contract, when the courts will later regard the term as an innominate term: *Cehave NV v Bremer Handelsgellschaft mbH (The Hansa Nord)* [1976] QB 44.

APPROACHING EXCLUSION CLAUSES

As we have seen above, a contract will include both express and implied terms. A contract may also include clauses that exclude liability in certain circumstances. You may have noticed that in car parks there are signs that attempt to exclude liability for any damage done to customers' cars; similarly, in workplaces the employer may put up signs to make his employees and visitors aware that he excludes liability for theft and lost property on work premises. We have seen that in a contract for the sale of goods, statute will imply terms stating that the goods must be of satisfactory quality, etc. The seller will not want to include these terms into the contract because if he is in breach, the innocent party will have the right to repudiate the contract. In non-consumer contracts, the seller may wish to exclude the implied terms completely and instead replace them with warranties. The seller might also wish to exclude liability for late delivery, negligence, etc.

Apart from exclusion clauses, a contract may contain a clause that limits the liability of the parties in an event of breach. These are known as limitation clauses. Limitation clauses will often exclude consequential losses such as loss of goodwill, and state the maximum amount that a party will be liable for.

Crucially, the party who has breached the contract and wishes to rely upon an exclusion clause must show three things: firstly, that the exclusion clause has been incorporated into the contract; secondly, that the clause covers the breach; and thirdly, that the clause is valid. This section of the chapter will explore:

- the common law principles relating to the incorporation of such clauses into a contract,
- the interpretation of exclusion clauses, and
- the rules relating to their validity under statute.

It should be noted that the rules relating to incorporation also apply to other terms; however, here we will be focusing on exclusion clauses.

INCORPORATION OF TERMS INTO A CONTRACT

A clause may be incorporated into a contract in one of three ways: by signature, by previous course of dealing or by notice.

Incorporation by signature

Where a person signs a written contract, he is bound by all of the terms within that contract. It is irrelevant whether he read the contract or not.

KEY CASE ANALYSIS: *L'Estrange v F Graucob Ltd* [1934] 2 KB 394

Background

The purchaser of a slot machine signed the sale agreement without reading it. The agreement contained a clause that excluded the liability of the seller in relation to the implied term that the machine would be fit for purpose. The issue arising was whether the exclusion clause had been incorporated into the contract.

Principle established

It was held that the exclusion clause had been incorporated into the contract for sale and thus the seller was not liable for breach of contract when the machine was not fit for purpose. Maugham LJ stated that he regretted his decision but felt bound by previous decisions. His Lordship commented that the terms were 'in regrettably small print but quite legible'.

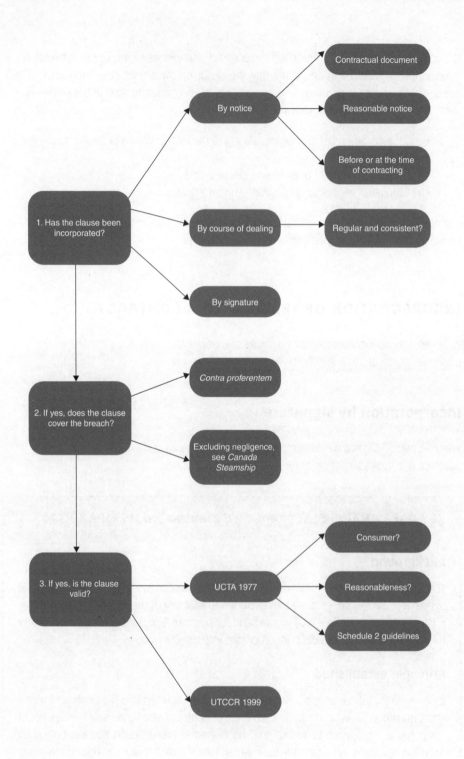

We will see later that where the court regards a clause to be onerous, the party relying upon that clause must take reasonable steps to bring the clause to the other party's attention; for example, by using larger font.

Even where an elderly lady had mislaid her glasses when she signed a contract, and thus did not read the terms but instead relied upon what someone told her the contract said, she was still held to be bound by the terms in the contract: *Saunders v Anglia Building Society* [1971] AC 1004.

There is a defence available to a party who signs a contractual agreement. This defence is known as *non est factum* and it applies where the party is illiterate. This is an historical defence, but it has been extended in recent years to 'those who are permanently or temporarily unable through no fault of their own to have without explanation any real understanding of the purport of a particular document, whether that be from defective education, illness or innate incapacity' (per Lord Reid in *Saunders*).

Incorporation by previous course of dealing

A term may also be incorporated into a contract where the parties have had a regular and consistent previous course of dealings: *McCutcheon v David MacBrayne Ltd* [1964] 1 WLR 125. The case of *Hollier v Rambler Motors (AMC) Ltd* [1972] 2 QB 71, illustrates that three or four transactions over a period of five years is not regular and consistent enough to constitute a course of dealing. However, 100 transactions in three years is sufficient to constitute a course of dealing: *Henry Kendall v William Lillico Ltd* [1969] 2 AC 31.

On-the-spot question

? Louise is shopping for a new sweatshirt. At the point of sale, there is a notice that states, 'No refunds at all are available on items purchased'. Louise buys the sweatshirt but after a week she notices that the stitching in the sleeves has become undone. She returns to the shop and the manager points to the notice and refuses to give her a refund.

Advise Louise as to whether there is a breach of contract and, if so, whether the exclusion clause has been incorporated.

Incorporation by notice

There are three requirements that must be satisfied before a term may be said to be incorporated into a contract by notice.

The term must be contained within a contractual document

In *Chapelton v Barry UDC* [1940] 1 KB 532, the claimant hired a deckchair and was given a ticket on payment. The ticket contained a clause that excluded liability for injury. The claimant was injured and the defendant sought to rely upon the exclusion clause. The court held that the clause had not been incorporated into the contract for hire because the ticket was a mere receipt and not a contractual document – it was not a document upon which you would expect to find contractual terms.

The term must have been brought to the other party's attention before or at the time of contracting

In *Olley v Marlborough Court Ltd* [1949] 1 KB 532, the claimant booked into a hotel and went up to her room. On the back of the door to the room there was a clause that excluded liability of the hotel for lost or stolen articles unless they had been deposited with the manageress for safe keeping. The claimant's fur coat was stolen and the defendant sought to rely upon the exclusion clause. The Court of Appeal held that the clause had not been incorporated into the contract because it had been brought to the claimant's attention only after contracting. The contract was formed at the reception desk and the clause was displayed in the bedroom.

KEY CASE ANALYSIS: *Thornton v Shoe Lane Parking Ltd* **[1971] 2 QB 163**

Background

The claimant parked in a car park that he had not used before. Whilst in the car park the claimant was severely injured in an accident. The defendant sought to argue that an exclusion clause had been incorporated into the contract through the ticket issued by the automatic machine.

Principle established

The Court of Appeal dismissed the defendant's appeal. Lord Denning MR held that if the claimant had read the ticket he would have been directed to where the list of conditions had been displayed; however, he could not have read these conditions

---

without first having parked his car. His Lordship rejected the argument that the clause had been incorporated before or at the time of contracting. The defendant's offer to park was accepted as soon as the claimant:

> drove up to the entrance and, by the movement of his car, turned the light from red to green, and the ticket was thrust at him. The contract was then concluded, and it could not be altered by any words printed on the ticket itself. In particular, it could not be altered so as to exempt the company from liability for personal injury due to their negligence.

Reasonable steps must have been taken to bring the term to the other party's attention.

The party relying on the term must take such steps as are reasonable to bring the term to the other party's attention, but it is not necessary to prove that the other party actually read the term: *Parker v South Eastern Railway* (1877) 2 CPD 416. In fact, it is irrelevant that the particular party against whom the term is being relied upon is physically unable to read the term: *Thompson v London, Midland and Scottish Railway* [1930] 1 KB 41.

It is also possible to incorporate a term by reference. For example, in *Thompson*, the claimant was given a ticket that stated 'For conditions see back'. There was writing on the back of a rail ticket that referred the reader to terms contained in another document (a relatively expensive railway timetable), which could be purchased. The term relied upon in this case was contained on page 552 of this timetable. It was nevertheless held to have been incorporated into the contract by reasonable notice.

Onerous terms

There is a further burden upon a party who seeks to rely upon an onerous term (i.e. a term that places a heavy burden on one party). That party must take more steps to bring the term to the other party's notice. Would a term be onerous if an employer could dock an employee a day's wage if that employee turned up 15 minutes late to work? The more onerous the term relied upon, the more steps that the party relying on the term must take to bring that term to the attention of the other party. This principle is known colloquially as the 'red hand rule' and was first propounded by Lord Denning (Denning LJ as he then was) in the case of *J Spurling Ltd v Bradshaw* [1956] 1 WLR 461, '. . . the more unreasonable a clause is, the greater the notice which must be given of it. Some clauses which I have seen would need to be printed in red ink on the face of the document with a red hand pointing to it before the notice could be held to be sufficient'. This principle was later applied in the case of *Interfoto Picture Library Ltd v Stiletto Visual Programmes Ltd* [1989] QB 433.

KEY CASE ANALYSIS: *Interfoto Picture Library Ltd v Stiletto Visual Programmes Ltd* [1989] QB 433

Background

The defendant had hired transparencies from the claimant. The contract stipulated that these should be returned with 14 days. The defendants were not accustomed to the claimant's terms and conditions and returned the transparencies late after four weeks. The fee charged for late delivery was extremely high and the claimants demanded £3,783.50. The issue was whether the clause containing the late delivery charge had been incorporated by reasonable notice.

Principle established

The Court of Appeal held that onerous terms must be adequately brought to the other parties' attention by taking more steps.

Bingham LJ stated that the duty the claimants owed the defendants was 'in essence a principle of fair and open dealing. In such a forum it might, I think, be held on the facts of this case that the plaintiffs were under a duty in all fairness to draw the defendants' attention specifically to the high price payable if the transparencies were not returned in time and, when the 14 days had expired, to point out to the defendants the high cost of continued failure to return them'.

CONSTRUCTION

After considering whether a clause is incorporated into a contract, the next question to ask is whether the clause covers the breach. According to *Anson's Law of Contract*, 'the words of the exemption clause must exactly cover the liability which it is sought to exclude' (Beatson, Burrows & Cartwright, 29th edn, OUP, p178). The strict approach taken by the courts is demonstrated in *Andrew Bros v Singer & Co Ltd* [1934] 1 KB 17. This case involved the sale of 'a new Singer car' (this was an express term). The defendant had attempted to exclude any terms that were implied into the contract by statute. The express term was breached as the car had done a considerable distance at the time of sale and thus was not 'new'. The defendant could not rely on the exclusion clause as this only covered implied terms and not express terms. Thus, the clause did not cover the breach.

The *contra proferentem* rule states that where there is any ambiguity, the clause was to be construed against the party seeking to rely on it. This means that a party who at a later date might wish to rely on an exclusion clause must ensure, firstly, that it covers any foreseeable breach, and secondly, that it is clearly worded.

Negligence

Where the clause attempts to exclude liability for negligence, then a three-stage test is applied. Lord Morton in the Privy Council in *Canada Steamship Lines Ltd v The King* [1952] AC 192 stated that the correct approach was, firstly, to ask whether there was any express language that excluded liability for negligence. If there was not, then the second question was whether 'the words used are wide enough, in their ordinary meaning, to cover negligence on the part of the servants of the *proferens*'. If they were not wide enough, then the clause would be construed against the party relying on it. Thirdly, 'If the words used are wide enough for the above purpose, the court must then consider whether "the head of damage may be based on some ground other than that of negligence"'. However, the other grounds should not be too remote or fanciful.

Limitation clauses

Whilst the *contra proferentem* rule does apply to limitation clauses, it is less strictly applied: *Ailsa Craig Fishing Co Ltd v Malvern Fishing Co Ltd and Securicor (Scotland) Ltd* [1983] 1 WLR 964. Lord Fraser acknowledged the strictness of the construction of exclusion clauses, but stated that 'these principles are not applicable in their full rigour when considering the effect of clauses merely limiting liability'. This is because a party is more likely to agree a limitation clause than a clause excluding liability in its entirety.

VALIDITY

Unfair Contract Terms Act 1977

Further controls on the application of exclusion clauses have been created by Parliament. The Unfair Contract Terms Act 1977 (UCTA 1977) regulates the use of exclusion clauses. Through this statute, Parliament has prevented parties from having complete freedom to contract. UCTA 1977 affords protection to consumers and businesses when contracting.

Who is a consumer?

A consumer is defined under s 12 UTCA 1977 as a party who does not make the contract in the course of a business, nor holds himself out as doing so. Section 12 is limited to contracts for those goods that are of a type ordinarily supplied for private use or consumption. This could include coffee, milk and a car, but would exclude a multi-million pound piece of machinery. Can businesses deal as a consumer under UCTA 1977? The answer is yes, so long as they comply with s 12. This is demonstrated by *R & B Customs Brokers Co Ltd v United Dominions Trust Ltd* [1988] 1 All ER 847. In this case, the claimants bought a car for one of their directors to use. The court held that the purchase was only incidental to the carrying on of their business, and the defendants had failed to show a degree of regularity on the part of the claimants. The purchase of the car was not an integral part of the claimants' business. Crucially, had the claimants regularly purchased cars and then sold these for a profit, they would not have been dealing as a consumer.

Excluding implied terms

Section 6 of UCTA 1977 prevents a business from excluding the terms implied by the SGA 1979 against a consumer. Section 6(1) states that s 12 SGA 1979 (implied term as to title) can never be excluded from any commercial contract (meaning business to business) or consumer contract. Section 6(2) UCTA 1977 states that ss 13–15 SGA 1979 can never be excluded from any consumer contract. Where the buyer is a non-consumer, s 6(3) UCTA 1977 states that ss 13–15 SGA 1979 can only be excluded if this is reasonable under s 11 (see below).

Section 3 of UCTA 1977 applies between contracting parties where one of them deals as a consumer or as a business contracting on the other's standard terms of business. This is to ensure that the party in the weaker bargaining position is not exploited. Section 3(2)(a) states that the party who is not dealing as a consumer, or who is contracting on their own standard terms of business, cannot exclude or restrict liability for his own breach of contract unless the contract term satisfies the requirement of reasonableness. Section 3(2)(b) states that the party in breach will only be entitled to (i) render a contractual performance that is substantially different from what was reasonably expected of him, or (ii) not fulfil his contractual obligation at all, if it satisfies the requirement of reasonableness.

Negligence

Under s 2(1) UCTA 1977 it is not possible to exclude liability for death and personal injury. This applies regardless of whether the parties are consumers or businesses. Section 2(2) states that a party can only exclude liability for negligence, for both consumer and commercial transactions, if he satisfies the requirement of reasonableness.

Reasonableness

In deciding whether a clause is reasonable, it is important to look at the test in s 11(1) UCTA 1977. This states that 'the term shall have been a fair and reasonable one to be included having regard to the circumstances which were, or ought reasonably to have been, known to or in the contemplation of the parties when the contract was made'. To assist in determining 'reasonableness' in relation to the implied terms under s 6(3) UCTA 1977, the court should have regard to any of the guidelines under Schedule 2 that appear to be relevant, namely:

(a) the strength of the bargaining positions of the parties relative to each other, taking into account (among other things) alternative means by which the customer's requirements could have been met;

(b) whether the customer received an inducement to agree to the term, or in accepting it had an opportunity of entering into a similar contract with other persons, but without having a similar term;

(c) whether the customer knew or ought reasonably to have known of the existence and the extent of the term (having regard, among other things, to any custom of the trade and any previous course of dealing between the parties);

(d) where the term excludes or restricts any relevant liability if some condition was not complied with, whether it was reasonable at the time of the contract to expect that compliance with that condition would be practicable;

(e) whether the goods were manufactured, processed or adapted to the special order of the customer.

However, according to Lord Bridge in *George Mitchell (Chesterhall) Ltd v Finney Lock Seeds Ltd* [1983] 2 AC 803, when considering the meaning of 'reasonableness' in relation to s 3 UCTA 1977, the court can make reference to the Schedule 2 guidelines. The court should also have regard to any other relevant circumstances, including resources and the ability to insure the goods. This approach was adopted by the Court of Appeal in *Overseas Medical Supplies Ltd v Orient Transport Services Ltd* [1999] 2 Lloyds Rep 273. In *Watford Electronics Ltd v Sanderson CFL* [2001] EWCA Civ 217, the Court of Appeal had to consider the validity of a clause that purported to limit liability. The court approved of the test in *George Mitchell* when considering reasonableness under s 3 and considered the Schedule 2 guidelines. The correct approach is to weigh up the factors that indicate whether the term is or is not reasonable. In *Watford Electronics* the court stated that, 'In circumstances in which parties of equal bargaining power negotiate a price for the supply of product under an agreement which provides for the person on whom the risk of loss will fall, it seems to me that the court should be very cautious before reaching the conclusion that the agreement which they have reached is not a fair and reasonable one' (*per* Peter Gibson LJ). Therefore, when businesses contract, there is a presumption that the exclusion clause is reasonable.

Unfair Terms in Consumer Contract Regulations 1999

The European Union have attempted to harmonise consumer protection and the Unfair Terms in Consumer Contract Regulations 1999 (UTCCR 1999) seek to restrict the use of unfair terms. These regulations apply not only to exclusion and limitation clauses, but more widely to any unfair term in a consumer contract. A term that has not been individually negotiated is deemed to be unfair under Regulation 5(1) if 'contrary to the requirement of good faith, it causes a significant imbalance in the parties' rights and obligations arising under the contract, to the detriment of the consumer'. Any written term must be expressed 'in plain, intelligible language' and any ambiguity is construed in the consumer's favour (Regulation 7). Under Regulation 8(1), any unfair terms in the contract are not binding on the consumer.

SUMMARY

- Statements that are intended to become part of the contract and be binding on the parties are terms of the contract which, if breached, would entitle the innocent party to repudiation and/or damages (breach of contract).
- Statements that are intended to induce the other to enter into the contract but which are not part of the contract are representations which, if false, could entitle the innocent party to rescission and/or damages (misrepresentation).
- In addition to the terms expressly agreed by the parties, terms may be implied into a contract by statute (e.g. the Sale of Goods Act 1979), the courts or by custom.

- Terms can be classified as conditions, warranties or innominate terms. If breached, a condition will give the innocent party the right to repudiate the contract and/or claim damages. Breach of warranty only provides the innocent party with the right to damages. Breach of an innominate term may be treated as either a breach of condition or breach of warranty depending upon the seriousness of the breach.
- Exemption clauses must be incorporated into a contract by signature, by reasonable notice before or at the time of contracting or by previous course of dealing. Such clauses must also be valid under the Unfair Contract Terms Act 1977 and the Unfair Terms in Consumer Contract Regulations 1999.

FURTHER READING

Macdonald E, 'The duty to give notice of unusual contract terms' [1988] JBL 375 – This article explores Lord Denning's 'red hand' rule, which applies to onerous terms. It looks at the case of *Interfoto* and assesses whether the rule has been made redundant by UCTA 1977.

Palmer NE, 'Limiting liability for negligence' [1982] 45 MLR 322 – This article questions the distinction drawn in *Ailsa Craig* between limitation clauses and exclusion clauses in relation to liability for negligence.

Peel E, 'Reasonable exemption clauses' [2001] 117 LQR 545 – This article is a case commentary on the decision of the Court of Appeal in *Watford Electronics*.

Spencer JR, 'Signature, Consent and the Rule in *L'Estrange v Graucob*' [1973] CLJ 104 – This article considers the three defences to the rule in *L'Estrange*, namely fraud, misrepresentation and *non est factum*.

Stone R, *The Modern Law of Contract*, 9th edn (Routledge, 2011) – Refer to this textbook for a more advanced consideration of the issues raised in this chapter.

Stone R, *Q&A Contract Law 2012–2013* (Routledge, 2012) – This book will help you to prepare for your exams.

COMPANION WEBSITE

An online glossary compiled by the authors is available on the companion website: www.routledge.com/cw/beginningthelaw

Chapter 5
Misrepresentation

LEARNING OUTCOMES

After reading this chapter, you should be able to:

- Define misrepresentation
- Explain the effects of a successful action for misrepresentation
- Understand which types of statements are actionable
- Demonstrate knowledge of the categories of misrepresentation
- Appreciate which remedies are available for the various types of misrepresentation

DEFINING MISREPRESENTATION

During the course of negotiations, contracting parties may make a number of statements to each other that neither party intends to become terms of the contract. These are representations and they are not binding on the parties, thus there is no action for breach of contract if they turn out to be false. Refer back to Chapter 4 for an explanation of the distinction between terms and representations. However, where a party (X) makes an unambiguous false representation of fact or law to another party (Y) and that statement **induces** Y to enter into a contract with X, causing loss to Y, may have an action in **misrepresentation**.

Key Definitions

The key requirements for an **actionable misrepresentation** are:

(1) False statement of fact or law
(2) Made to another party
(3) Induces that party to contract with you

False statement of fact or law **+** Made to other contracting party **+** Inducement **=** Actionable misrepresentation

EFFECT OF MISREPRESENTATION

Misrepresentation makes the contract voidable

It is important to note the effect of an actionable misrepresentation: it will make the contract voidable and not void. Where a contract is void, the contract is treated as if it never existed and all obligations under it disappear. On the other hand, where a contract is voidable, the contract continues to exist and the parties must perform their obligations until the innocent party asks the court to rescind the contract. As we shall see below, rescission is not automatic and will be granted at the court's discretion.

Key Definitions

Void – Where a contract is void, it is deemed not to have been created in the first place.

Voidable – Where a contract is voidable, it is deemed to have been created, but the innocent party may choose to rescind the contract.

Remedies

Where an action for misrepresentation is successful, the innocent party may claim damages and/or rescind the contract (depending upon the category of misrepresentation).

Key Definition

Rescission – This is a remedy available where a contract is deemed to be voidable. The innocent party may choose to rescind (terminate) the contract or to affirm it.

The purpose of an award of damages for misrepresentation is to put the innocent party into the position that they would have been in had the misrepresentation been true. Thus, this protects the expectation interest of the innocent party. Refer to Chapter 10 on remedies for a fuller discussion of damages and expectation interest.

NATURE OF STATEMENT

Not all false statements made during contractual negotiations will lead to a successful action for misrepresentation. It is important to consider the nature of the false statement to determine whether the statement is actionable or not. We have seen from the definition above that a misrepresentation is a false statement of fact or law. Below, we will explore which statements are actionable misrepresentations and those types of statement that are not actionable.

Silence

It is important to note firstly that there is generally no duty to disclose information to someone who you are contracting with (although there are some exceptions to this rule, notably in cases involving contracts *uberrimae fidei*, or contracts 'of the utmost good faith', such as insurance contracts).

Silence is not grounds for an action in misrepresentation (*Keates v The Earl of Cadogan* (1851) 10 CB 591) because, according to the principle of freedom of contract, each contracting party is responsible for protecting his own interests. Contract law is reluctant to allow a party who has entered into a bad bargain to escape from his obligations under the contract. In the context of contracts for the sale of goods, this is often summarised by the principle *caveat emptor* (or 'buyer beware'). For example, if you are selling a computer and you do not disclose to the buyer that it crashes frequently and is slow to start up, you cannot be sued for misrepresentation when the buyer discovers those faults after the sale (although there may be a potential action for breach of contract). However, there is only no action for misrepresentation if no statement (whether by words or conduct) has been made. So, if the seller asks you whether the computer is slow to start up and you say 'no' in response, or you say nothing but shake your head, this will amount to a statement of fact (by words in the first instance and by conduct in the second).

On-the-spot question

Why do you think that the law imposes no duty to disclose information between contracting parties?

Conduct

As we have seen above, a false statement of fact may be made by conduct, and thus conduct may be an actionable misrepresentation if it induces the other party to enter into the contract. In *Walters v Morgan* (1861) 3 DF & G 718, it was stated that 'a nod or a wink, or a shake of the head, or a smile', which was intended to induce the other party to enter into the contract, was an actionable misrepresentation. Misrepresentation by conduct can also be seen in the case of *Spice Girls Ltd v Aprilia World Service BV* [2002] EWCA Civ 15, in which the members of the pop group, the Spice Girls, made representations by conduct that they each were unaware that any member intended to leave the group before the end of a sponsorship agreement. The conduct that formed the basis of the misrepresentation was participating in a commercial photo shoot. However, the members of the group knew at the time of the photo shoot that one member did intend to leave the group before the end of the agreement.

'Mere puff'

Mere advertising puff or sales talk is not actionable. In *Dimmock v Hallett* (1866–67) LR 2 Ch App 21, the description of land as 'fertile and improvable' was mere puff and there was no action for misrepresentation when the buyer realised that the land was useless. Other examples of mere puffs include the slogan currently used to advertise the energy drink, Red Bull, which is 'Red Bull gives you wings', and the slogan used to advertise the antiperspirant for men, Lynx, which suggests that the user will be irresistible to girls. These are clearly mere advertising puffs because they are not expected to be believed, and thus they are not actionable. However, the more specific such a statement is, the more likely it is that it will be treated as an actionable statement of fact.

Opinion

Generally speaking, a false statement of opinion made during contractual negotiations is not an actionable misrepresentation: *Bisset v Wilkinson* [1927] AC 177. In this case, Bisset was selling land in New Zealand to Wilkinson. Wilkinson planned to use the land for sheep farming. Both parties knew that the land had not previously been used for sheep farming, but Bisset stated that he thought that the land had the capacity to carry 2,000 sheep. However, it transpired that the land could not carry 2,000 sheep and Wilkinson argued that the contract should be rescinded due to the misrepresentation made by Bisset. The Privy Council held that the statement made by Bisset was an honestly held statement of opinion, which was not actionable. By contrast, where an opinion is not honestly held, it is a false statement of fact of that person's opinion, and thus is an actionable misrepresentation: *Edgington v Fitzmaurice* (1885) LR 29 Ch D 459.

Both parties in *Bisset v Wilkinson* knew that the land had never previously been used for sheep farming, but where only one party is aware of the facts, then a statement of opinion by that party may be actionable as a statement of fact since 'he impliedly states that he knows facts which justify his opinion' (per Bowen LJ in *Smith v Land and House Property Corporation* (1884) 28 Ch D 7). In *Smith v Land and House Property Corporation*, Smith was selling property at an auction that he stated was let to 'a most desirable tenant'. In fact, the tenant did not have a good record for paying rent on time. It was held that the statement was an actionable misrepresentation since Smith was the only one with knowledge of these facts and he had no reasonable grounds for the opinion. It was an untrue assertion that nothing had occurred to make the tenant undesirable.

The principle that expertise or special knowledge may elevate a statement of opinion to an actionable misrepresentation has been confirmed in the case of *Esso Petroleum Co Ltd v Mardon* [1976] QB 801. Thus, where a statement of opinion is made during contractual negotiations by a person who has special expertise or knowledge in the matter and the statement is false, it may lead to an action for misrepresentation if it induces the other party to enter into the contract.

KEY CASE ANALYSIS: *Esso Petroleum Co Ltd v Mardon* [1976] QB 801

Background

Mardon took the lease of a new petrol station after being assured by a representative from Esso that the station would do well, reaching an annual 'throughput' of 200,000 gallons of petrol per year. However, the layout of the petrol station meant that this figure was never reached. Mardon claimed that Esso had made a negligent misrepresentation. Esso argued that this was a statement of opinion since there had not previously been a petrol station on that site.

Principle established

The Court of Appeal held that a statement of opinion could be elevated to a statement of fact by expertise and special knowledge. Here, the statement was one of fact because Esso had expertise and special knowledge of the sales of petrol at petrol stations in various locations. Thus, the statement was an actionable misrepresentation.

Statement of law

A false statement of law made during contractual negotiations is also an actionable misrepresentation if it induces the other contracting party to enter into the contract. This is a recent development to the law because previously there was a distinction between false statements of fact that were actionable and false statements of law that were not. However, in *Kleinwort Benson Ltd v Lincoln City Council* [1999] 2 AC 349, a case on mistake, the House of Lords held that there should be no distinction between mistakes of law and mistakes of fact, and in *Pankhania v London Borough of Hackney* [2002] EWHC 2441 (Ch), the High Court confirmed that the same principle should apply to misrepresentation. Thus, false statements of law may form the basis of an actionable misrepresentation.

Statement of future intention

Generally speaking, a false statement of future intention is not actionable for misrepresentation provided that the maker of the statement honestly held that intention at the time that they made the statement: *Wales v Wadham* [1977] 1 WLR 199. However, if the intention is not honestly held at the time of making the statement, then the maker is misrepresenting his intention, which is a misrepresentation of fact and is actionable: *Edgington v Fitzmaurice* (1885) LR 29 Ch D 459. According to Bowen LJ: 'The state of a man's mind is as much a matter of fact as the state of his digestion . . . A misrepresentation as to the state of a man's mind is, therefore, a misstatement of fact.'

Change of circumstances

We have already stated that there is generally no duty on a contracting party to disclose information to the other party. However, one exception to this rule arises where a change of circumstances relating to a representation has already been made and which was true when it was made, but later become false. If there is such a change of circumstances, then there is a duty on the representor to correct the representation previously made: *With v O'Flanagan* [1936] Ch 575.

KEY CASE ANALYSIS: *With v O'Flanagan* [1936] Ch 575

Background

O'Flanagan was selling his medical practice and made a statement that the takings were £2,000 per annum. At the time that the statement was made this was true.

However, O'Flanagan later fell ill, which caused the practice to decline, such that when he did sell the practice, the takings were much lower. O'Flanagan did not disclose this change of circumstances to the buyer, With, who sought to rescind the contract on the basis of misrepresentation.

Principle established

The Court of Appeal held that the failure to declare to the buyer that the change in circumstances now rendered the original representation about the takings untrue, was an actionable misrepresentation.

Half-truths

Half-truths are a further exception to the general rule that silence is not actionable. A half-truth is a statement that may be true in some respects and on a literal interpretation, but is misleading in that it hides an untruth. McKendrick terms a half-truth as a 'statement [which] is literally true but is nevertheless misleading' (*Contract Law*, 9th edn, Palgrave at p217). Half-truths are actionable misrepresentations. An example of a half-truth is provided by *Dimmock v Hallett* (1866–67) LR 2 Ch App 21, in which the seller of land described the land as in occupation by a tenant for £290. These facts were true, but the seller failed to disclose that the tenant had given notice to quit and that the new tenant was to pay a lower rent. Another example of a half-truth would be if a supermarket were to advertise a range of bananas on the basis that they had been voted by customers as 'the best bananas ever to have been grown in the village of Sarratt in Hertfordshire'. If the bananas had indeed been grown in Sarratt, Hertfordshire, then this statement would literally be true, but it would only be half-true if the bananas were the only bananas ever to have been grown in Sarratt, Hertfordshire.

On-the-spot question

 Consider whether the following statements are actionable misrepresentations or not:

(i)   A dating website advertises its service: 'We believe in happy every after. Find your fairy tale love with your knight in shining armour.'

(ii) You ask your accountant to look over the accounts of a restaurant you are considering buying. He tells you, 'In my opinion, it is a solid investment.' After buying the restaurant, you find out that it is not profitable.

(iii) You are offered a job at a company and told that there is an annual work weekend away to Las Vegas, all expenses paid by the company. However, before you accept the job, the weekend away is cancelled due to the economic crisis.

(iv) You decide to rent a flat from a landlord after he informs you that in six months' time he plans to install a communal swimming pool for residents' use. However, after six months there is still no swimming pool.

INDUCEMENT

It is not enough that a false statement of fact or law is simply made to the other contracting party, but the false statement must also **induce** the other party into entering into the contract. According to *Edgington v Fitzmaurice* (1885) LR 29 Ch D 459, the statement need not be the sole inducement that led the party to enter into the contract. However, it must certainly be an inducement: *JEB Fasteners Ltd v Marks Bloom & Co* [1983] 1 All ER 583.

KEY CASE ANALYSIS: *JEB Fasteners Ltd v Marks Bloom & Co* [1983] 1 All ER 583

Background

The defendants in this case were the auditors of a company (BG Fasteners), which JEB Fasteners was considering taking over. The defendants had negligently prepared accounts that JEB Fasteners Ltd knew were not completely accurate at the time of contracting. However, the takeover went ahead because JEB Fasteners wanted to acquire the services of the two directors who worked for BG Fasteners. The accounts were substantially inaccurate and JEB Fasteners lost a lot of money as a result of the takeover. JEB Fasteners brought an action for negligent misstatement against the defendants.

Principle established

The action was not successful as JEB Fasteners had purchased the firm in order to acquire the directors of BG Fasteners, and they had not been induced by the accounts.

The Court of Appeal considered the issue of inducement. Stephenson LJ held that:

> . . . the cause of action is the same as in all claims for damages for misrepresentation. The misrepresentation must be false, and it must induce

the plaintiff to act upon it to his detriment. If he does, he relies on it; if he does not, he does not. He may, of course, rely on other things as well. What operates on his mind, or motivates him, or influences him to act as he does, may be a number of things, some operating more or less strongly . . .

There can be no inducement where the claimant was entirely unaware of the false representation, as in *Horsfall v Thomas* (1862) 1 H & C 90, in which Horsfall made a cannon for sale to Thomas. The cannon had a defect that was concealed by Horsfall and that Thomas did not find until he fired the cannon. The concealment of the defect was held not to have induced Thomas since he knew nothing of the defect until after the contract had been concluded.

There is also no inducement, and thus no misrepresentation, where the claimant has not relied on the false statement of fact or law made: *Attwood v Small* (1838) 6 Cl & F 232.

KEY CASE ANALYSIS: *Attwood v Small* (1838) 6 Cl & F 232, HL

Background

Attwood sold a mine to Small (and other joint purchasers). Attwood had made a number of statements about the capabilities of the mine, and the purchasers appointed some agents to check the truth of the statements. The agents reported back, verifying the statements made by Attwood. However, the statements later turned out to be false and the purchasers sought to rescind the contract on the ground of misrepresentation.

Principle established

The House of Lords held that there was no misrepresentation in this case because the statements had not induced the purchasers to enter into the contract. In fact, the purchasers had tested those statements by appointing agents and they relied upon the agents' verifications.

Burden of proof

In *Museprime Properties Ltd v Adhill Properties Ltd* (1991) 61 P & CR 111, Scott J adopted the approach taken by Lord Goff and Professor Jones on *The Law of Restitution* (3rd edn, Sweet and Maxwell at p 168) in relation to proving inducement:

> If the misrepresentation would have induced a reasonable person to enter into the contract then the court will...presume that the representee was so induced and the onus will be on the representor to show that the representee did not rely on the misrepresentation either wholly or in part. If, however, the misrepresentation would not have induced a reasonable person to contract, the onus will be on the representee to show that the misrepresentation induced him to act as he did.

Thus, the approach is:

(1)   if a reasonable person would have been induced to enter into the contract, the burden is on the representor to prove that the representee was in fact not induced;

(2)   if a reasonable person would not have been induced to enter into the contract, the burden is on the representee to prove that they were in fact induced.

Requirement of materiality

Misrepresentation requires that the false statement of fact or law be material, but it is not entirely clear whether this is a separate requirement to the requirement of inducement. The courts seem to have treated materiality as though it was the same as the requirement that the statement induces the other party to enter into the contract. Thus, in *Museprime Properties Ltd v Adhill Properties Ltd*, Scott J stated that: 'A representation is material . . . if it is something that induces the person to whom it is made, whether solely or in conjunction with other inducements, to contract on the terms on which he does contract.'

Opportunity to check

Where the claimant is given the opportunity to check the truth of the statement made, for example, by inspecting the property or goods, he may still bring an action for misrepresentation even if he does not take the opportunity to make any checks: *Redgrave v Hurd* (1881–82) LR 20 Ch D 1.

KEY CASE ANALYSIS: *Redgrave v Hurd* (1881–82) LR 20 Ch D 1

Background

The claimant was a solicitor who wanted to take on a partner in his practice and sell his house. The claimant informed the defendant that his practice brought in about £300 per year and after enquiry by the defendant, the claimant produced summaries of transactions valued at just under £200 per year. The claimant then showed the defendant other papers that he said represented the remaining £100 shortfall per year. The defendant did not inspect these papers but contracted with the claimant. In fact, the true income of the company was about £200 per year and the defendant later claimed rescission of the contract on grounds of misrepresentation.

Principle established

The Court of Appeal held that the claimant had no defence in the argument that the defendant had had the opportunity to inspect the documents, and the contract was rescinded.

It has been suggested that where it is reasonable for the claimant to take the opportunity to check the truth of the statement and he fails to make use of that opportunity, he should have no claim in misrepresentation (see Peel, *Treitel on The Law of Contract*, 12th edn, para 9-020). This arises from the House of Lords' authority, *Smith v Eric S Bush* [1990] 1 AC 831, HL, which involved a purchaser of a property who failed to have his own survey done, instead relying on the survey carried out on behalf of the mortgage company. The claimant failed in his action for negligent misstatement.

On-the-spot question

 Which of the following examples would amount to inducement?

- The sales particulars of a house state that the house has a 60-foot swimming pool. The purchaser only wishes to purchase the property because it is a good location to build a block of flats. In reality, the pool is 25 foot.
- The accounts that were prepared for the sale of a pub state that the pub made £67,000 profit last year. The purchaser was offered an opportunity to check the accounts, but refused. In fact, the pub only made £23,000 profit last year.

CATEGORIES OF MISREPRESENTATION

There are three different possible categories of misrepresentation:

- fraudulent misrepresentation;
- negligent misrepresentation; and
- innocent misrepresentation.

Each category will be discussed in turn.

Fraudulent misrepresentation

An action for fraudulent misrepresentation at common law is based upon the tort of deceit.

Proving fraud

KEY CASE ANALYSIS: *Derry v Peek* (1889) LR 14 App Cas 337, HL

Background

In this case, the directors of a company were sued by a shareholder who had purchased shares in their company based upon a prospectus, in which the directors had stated that their company had the right to use steam power instead of horses for its trams. Permission to use steam was refused.

Principle established

The House of Lords held that the defendants were not liable in the tort of deceit because they honestly believed that the statement was true.

Lord Herschell provided the test for deceit, which must today be satisfied to establish that a misrepresentation was fraudulent:

> I think the authorities establish the following propositions: First, in order to sustain an action of deceit, there must be proof of fraud, and nothing short of that will suffice. Secondly, fraud is proved when it is shewn that a false representation has been made (1) knowingly, or (2) without belief in its truth, or (3) recklessly, careless whether it be true or false. Although I have treated the second and third as distinct cases, I think the third is but an instance of the second, for one who makes a statement under such

circumstances can have no real belief in the truth of what he states. To prevent a false statement being fraudulent, there must, I think, always be an honest belief in its truth. And this probably covers the whole ground, for one who knowingly alleges that which is false has obviously no such honest belief. Thirdly, if fraud be proved, the motive of the person guilty of it is immaterial. It matters not that there was no intention to cheat or injure the person to whom the statement was made.

We can see from the quote above that it is very difficult for the claimant to prove that the defendant has made a fraudulent misrepresentation. The claimant has the burden of proof and must show, on a balance of probabilities, that the defendant made the fraudulent statement:

(1) knowingly, or
(2) without belief in its truth, or
(3) recklessly, careless of whether it is true or false.

The remedies available for fraudulent misrepresentation are damages and rescission, which are discussed below.

Measure of damages

Where it has been proved that the defendant made a fraudulent representation, the claimant may be awarded the tortious measure of damages in respect of the losses that he suffered. This measure of damages is designed to put the claimant back in the position he was before he entered into the contract. The case of *Doyle v Olby (Ironmongers) Ltd* [1969] 2 QB 158 provides that the amount of damages to be awarded to the claimant is widely construed to cover all losses that flow directly from the fraud, whether foreseeable or not.

KEY CASE ANALYSIS: *Doyle v Olby (Ironmongers) Ltd* [1969] 2 QB 158

Background

The buyer of a business alleged that the sellers had made a number of fraudulent misrepresentations, which related to a much lower turnover than stated and the fact that the company's trade was carried out at its premises. In reality, half the trade had been obtained by a travelling salesman. The buyer purchased the business and found out about the travelling salesman. However, he could not afford to employ a travelling salesman and then faced competition from another company associated with the sellers. The buyer sued the seller and obtained £1,500 damages. He then appealed to the Court of Appeal to obtain higher damages.

Principle established

Lord Denning MR stated that the trial judge had assessed the damages as if this was a contractual action, and reiterated that the calculation of damages is different for fraud than for contract:

> In fraud, the defendant has been guilty of a deliberate wrong by inducing the plaintiff to act to his detriment. The object of damages is to compensate the plaintiff for all the loss he has suffered, so far, again, as money can do it. In contract, the damages are limited to what may reasonably be supposed to have been in the contemplation of the parties. In fraud, they are not so limited. The defendant is bound to make reparation for all the actual damages directly flowing from the fraudulent inducement.

Therefore, unlike in contract, there was no requirement to mitigate losses in fraud. The claimant was awarded £5,500.

In *East v Maurer* [1991] 1 WLR 461, the Court of Appeal held that the claimant could recover all actual losses suffered and any loss of profits that reasonably could have been anticipated. It is clear that the measure of damages awarded for fraudulent misrepresentation is more generous than those usually recoverable in contract, thus there are advantages in suing for deceit rather than in contract. This generous measure of damages is intended to act as a deterrent to dissuade contracting parties from wilfully deceiving each other.

Rescission

As discussed above, a misrepresentation (no matter what category it is) will make the contract voidable. It is at the discretion of the court as to whether to set the contract aside using the remedy of rescission. However, it must be remembered that rescission is not an automatic remedy. There are four bars to rescission; in other words, rescission will not be granted in the following four circumstances:

1	Lapse of time
2	Impossible to return the parties to their original position
3	Third-party interests
4	Affirmation

In *Leaf v International Galleries* [1950] 2 KB 86, the court held that rescission was not available as a remedy because of the lapse of time between the misrepresentation and the claim. The claim was time-barred because five years had passed before the claimant realised the defendant had innocently misrepresented that the painting he had purchased was by Constable. Lord Evershed MR took the view that five years was more than enough time to find fault with the painting.

Rescission will not be available when it is no longer possible to return the parties to their original position. In *Thomas Witter v TBP Industries Ltd* [1996] 2 All ER 573, the court held that too many significant changes had been made to the business, and consequentially, rescission was no longer available as a remedy. Rescission was also not available because of third-party interests that would have been affected.

Finally, rescission will not be available as a remedy where the claimant has affirmed the misrepresentation. In *Long v Lloyd* [1958] 1 WLR 753, the claimant purchased a lorry and found out it was faulty. The defendant had made an innocent misrepresentation that the lorry was in 'excellent condition'. The Court of Appeal held that the remedy of rescission was not available because the claimant had accepted the defendant's offer to contribute towards the cost of repairs and had continued to use the lorry for its business.

Negligent misrepresentation

An action for negligent misrepresentation may be brought in contract law under s 2(1), Misrepresentation Act 1967 or in the tort of negligence at common law.

Misrepresentation under s 2(1), Misrepresentation Act 1967

An action to recover damages for negligent misrepresentation falls under s 2(1), Misrepresentation Act 1967. In order to recover under this section, there must be a contract between the party making the false representation and the party who was induced to enter into the contract and suffered loss as a result.

According to s 2(1), '[w]here a person has entered into a contract after a misrepresentation has been made to him by another party thereto and as a result thereof he has suffered loss, then, if the person making the misrepresentation would be liable to damages in respect thereof had the misrepresentation been made fraudulently, that person shall be so liable notwithstanding that the misrepresentation was not made fraudulently, unless he proves that he had reasonable ground to believe and did believe up to the time the contract was made the facts represented were true'.

A defendant will be liable for negligent misrepresentation unless he proves that:

(i)   he had reasonable grounds to believe that the facts represented were true, and

(ii)   he did believe that the facts represented were true.

Thus, in an action under s 2(1), Misrepresentation Act 1967, it is not necessary for the claimant to prove that there is a special relationship between the parties that imposes a duty of care (as is required for negligent misstatement at common law), but rather, there is a lesser onus of proof on the claimant. The claimant must prove that there was a misrepresentation, but the burden then shifts to the defendant to prove, on a balance of probabilities, that he had reasonable grounds to believe, and did believe, that the representation was true: *Howard Marine & Dredging Co Ltd v A Ogden & Sons (Excavations) Ltd* [1978] QB 574. If the defendant is unable to prove this, then he is liable for negligent misrepresentation, but if he does discharge this burden of proof, then the misrepresentation is an innocent one. An action under s 2(1) is a preferable one for a claimant since it imposes a greater onus on the defendant.

If a defendant is liable for negligent misrepresentation under s 2(1), Misrepresentation Act 1967, then the remedies available to the claimant are the same as are available for fraudulent misrepresentation, namely rescission and damages. An action under s 2(1), Misrepresentation Act 1967 is also preferable for a claimant because the measure of damages is the same generous award that is available for fraudulent misrepresentation at common law, namely the tortious measure of damages recoverable in the tort of deceit, which covers all losses that flow directly from the misrepresentation, whether foreseeable or not. Thus, the defendant who is liable for negligent misrepresentation is liable to the same extent as if he had fraudulently misrepresented the fact; this is known as the 'fiction of fraud'.

KEY CASE ANALYSIS: *Royscot Trust Ltd v Rogerson* [1991] 2 QB 297

Background

This case involved a car dealer who sold a car on hire purchase to a customer for £7,600 (deposit of £1,200 paid upfront), but the dealer misrepresented to the finance company that the cost of the car was £8,000 (deposit of £1,600). The finance company entered into the hire-purchase agreement with the customer on the misrepresentation that the deposit paid was 20% of the purchase price. The customer dishonestly sold the car and stopped paying the hire-purchase instalments. The finance company sued the car dealer for misrepresentation under s 2(1), Misrepresentation Act 1967.

Principle established

The Court of Appeal applied the tortious measure of damages and held that the finance company could recover the unpaid instalments from the car dealer, irrespective of whether the sale of the car by the customer was foreseeable or not.

Balcombe LJ stated that:

> . . . it seems to me that to suggest that a different measure of damage applies . . . is to ignore the plain words of the subsection and is inconsistent with the cases to which I have referred. In my judgment, therefore, the finance company is entitled to recover from the dealer all the losses which it suffered as a result of its entering into the agreements with the dealer and the customer, even if those losses were unforeseeable, provided that they were not otherwise too remote.

As stated above, rescission is available as a remedy for all types of misrepresentation. Rescission and the four bars to rescission have been discussed in detail above.

On-the-spot question

 What are the advantages of pursuing an action in negligent misrepresentation under s 2(1), Misrepresentation Act 1967, rather than fraudulent misrepresentation at common law?

Negligent misstatement at common law

Misrepresentation under s 2(1), Misrepresentation Act 1967 must be distinguished from an action for negligent misstatement at common law. Negligent misstatement at common law is based upon the tort of negligence and requires proof of a special relationship: *Hedley Byrne & Co Ltd v Heller & Partners Ltd* [1964] AC 465.

KEY CASE ANALYSIS: *Hedley Byrne & Co Ltd v Heller & Partners Ltd* [1964] AC 465, HL

Background

The appellants were an advertising agent who had placed substantial orders for advertising space for a company for which the appellants were financially liable. The appellants asked their banker to make inquiries into the financial status of the company. The banker made inquiries with the respondents, who were company's bankers. The respondents vouched for the creditworthiness of the company (although they did so 'without responsibility') and, on the basis of this reference, the appellants did not cancel the orders for advertising space. The company went into liquidation and the appellants lost £17,000. The appellants sued the respondents in negligence in order to recover the money lost.

The judge at first instance and the Court of Appeal held that there could be no action in the absence of a contractual relationship here, and that there was no special relationship that gave rise to a duty of care. The appellants appealed to the House of Lords.

Principle established

The House held that the claimants could not recover their losses on the grounds that the defendants had included a disclaimer that their references were given 'without responsibility'. However, the House significantly extended the scope of negligent misrepresentation by stating that if there had been no such disclaimer, the defendants would have been liable.

The House held that a claimant is able to recover damages in respect of a negligent misrepresentation where there was no contractual relationship, provided that it can be proved that there was a 'special relationship' between the parties. Where the claimant proves that there was a special relationship, the law will imply a duty of care on the party making the representation to exercise care and skill in making the statement. There is a 'special relationship' between the parties where the maker of the statement had special skill or knowledge, and it was reasonably foreseeable that the other party would rely on his statement.

Thus, a claimant may pursue an action in tort for negligent misstatement at common law even where there is no contractual relationship between him and the maker of the statement. The requirements of what needs to be proved to establish a special relationship has been the subject of much varying judicial opinion, but this is beyond the scope of this textbook.

Once a special relationship has been established, the claimant must also prove that the defendant was negligent in making the statement (i.e. that he failed to take reasonable care that the representation he made was true).

Table 5.1: Summary of available remedies

	Fraudulent misrepresentation at common law	Negligent misrepresentation under s 2(1), MA 1967	Negligent misstatement at common law	Innocent misrepresentation
Cause of action	Tort of deceit	Contract	Tort of negligence	Contract
Elements	False representation has been made (1) knowingly, or (2) without belief in its truth, or (3) recklessly, careless of whether it be true or false	Defendant had reasonable grounds to believe, and did believe, that the representation was true	That there was a special relationship between the parties and that the defendant failed to take reasonable care that the representation he made was true	Representation honestly held
Burden of proof	On claimant	On defendant to prove not negligent	On claimant	On defendant
Rescission available?	Yes	Yes	Yes	Yes
Measure of damages	All losses that flow directly from the fraud, whether foreseeable or not	All losses that flow directly from the misrepresentation, whether foreseeable or not	Reasonably foreseeable losses	Discretionary damages available in lieu or rescission

On-the-spot question

When would you use negligent misstatement at common law instead of negligent misrepresentation?

Where a defendant is liable for negligent misstatement at common law, the remedies available to the claimant are the same as those available for fraudulent misrepresentation, namely rescission and damages. The measure of damages available for negligent misstatement at common law is the tortious measure, but it is less generous than the measure of damages available for fraudulent misrepresentation in that a claimant may only recover for losses that are reasonably foreseeable. The bars to rescission that were discussed above also apply.

Innocent misrepresentation

Where the defendant has made a misrepresentation but he is neither fraudulent nor negligent, he may be liable for innocent misrepresentation. Rescission is available as a remedy for innocent misrepresentation, although the bars to rescission discussed above also apply. However, the claimant has no right to claim damages for innocent misrepresentation. Instead, the court has a statutory discretion to award damages in lieu of rescission under s 2(2), Misrepresentation Act 1967.

EXCLUDING LIABILITY FOR MISREPRESENTATION

A contracting party may exclude liability for a misrepresentation by including an exclusion clause in the contract. The exclusion clause will be treated like any other exclusion clause and it will be subject to the rules of incorporation and construction (refer back to Chapter 4 for these). Section 3 of the Misrepresentation Act 1967 provides a control on the use of such exclusion clauses by requiring that the clause is subject to the reasonableness test under s 11(1), Unfair Contract Terms Act 1977. Thus, it is for the person seeking to rely on the clause excluding or limiting liability for a misrepresentation to prove that the clause was incorporated into the contract, covers the misrepresentation and was reasonable under s 11(1), Unfair Contract Terms Act 1977.

SUMMARY

- Where a party makes an unambiguous false representation of fact or law to another party and that statement induces him to enter into a contract, he may have an action in misrepresentation which, if successful, may render the contract voidable (rescission) and allow the innocent party to claim damages.
- There are three categories of misrepresentation: fraudulent, negligent (including negligent misstatement at common law) and innocent. Each differs in terms of who bears the burden of proof and available remedies.
- Rescission is an equitable remedy that may be awarded at the discretion of the court. There are four bars to rescission: lapse of time, impossible to return the parties to their original position, third-party interests and affirmation.

FURTHER READING

Atiyah PS and Trietel G, 'Misrepresentation Act 1967' (1967) 30 MLR 369 – The authoritative article on the Misrepresentation Act 1967 and its implications for the law of contract.

Hooley R, 'Damages and the Misrepresentation Act 1967' (1991) 107 LQR 547 – This article provides case commentary on the decision in *Royscot Trust Ltd v Rogerson* [1991] 2 QB 297.

Koh P, 'Some issues in misrepresentation' [2008] 2 JBL 123 – This article looks at the requirements for an actionable misrepresentation, including the question of whether the misrepresentation needs to be material and whether inducement needs to be proved in cases of innocent misrepresentation.

Morgan P and Thompson T, 'Misrepresentation Minefield' (2012) 23(3) Construction Law 32 – This article considers the implications of potential misrepresentation that might be made by a mediator during the course of alternative dispute resolution.

Poole J and Devenney J, 'Reforming damages for misrepresentation: the case for coherent aims and principles' [2007] JBL 269 – This article explores the basis on which damages are awarded for misrepresentation and argues that the principles underlying the award of damages lack coherence and require clarification.

COMPANION WEBSITE

An online glossary compiled by the authors is available on the companion website: www.routledge.com/cw/beginningthelaw

Chapter 6
Mistake

LEARNING OUTCOMES

After reading this chapter, you should be able to:

- Distinguish between communication mistake and common mistake
- Appreciate that the doctrine of mistake is very narrowly applied
- Understand the circumstances in which mistake will affect the obligations under a contract
- Evaluate the distinction drawn between face-to-face and at a distance negotiations in cases on unilateral mistake as to identity
- Demonstrate knowledge of the law relating to common mistake

INTRODUCTION

This chapter explores the situations in which a contract may be regarded as **void** or as **negating consent** in light of mistakes that have been made by one or both of the parties to the contract. There are actually several doctrines of mistake, but they are all very narrowly or rarely applied. This means that in general it is very difficult for one or both parties to a contract to escape from their obligations under that agreement on grounds of mistake. There are two main types of mistake: **communication mistake** (also known as agreement mistake) and **common mistake**.

Key Definitions

Communication mistake – Where the parties never reached an agreement in the first place.

Common mistake – Where the parties did reach an agreement but both are mistaken about something fundamental that goes to the root of the contract.

COMMUNICATION MISTAKE

Communication mistake is also known as agreement mistake, and where this occurs the parties are deemed never to have reached an agreement in the first place. This type of mistake is based upon the principles of offer and acceptance that you considered in Chapter 2. Communication mistake may occur where both parties make a mistake when forming the agreement, such that they are talking at cross-purposes – this is known as **mutual mistake**. The other type of communication mistake occurs where just one of the parties makes a mistake when forming the agreement and the other party to the contract takes advantage of that mistake – this is known as **unilateral mistake**. Both of these types of communication mistake are considered below.

Key Definitions

Mutual mistake – Where the parties are negotiating at cross-purposes.

Unilateral mistake – Where one party takes advantage of the other's mistake.

Mutual mistake

Mutual mistake occurs where, when forming the agreement, the contracting parties are talking at cross-purposes. No agreement is reached because there is no meeting of the minds (no *consensus ad idem*), since the acceptance did not mirror the offer. However, mutual mistake will only render a contract void where the mistake is fundamental, such as a mistake as to the subject matter of the contract (*Raffles v Wichelhaus* (1864) 2 Hurl & C 906). If the mutual mistake is merely about a secondary characteristic and not something fundamental to the contract, then the mistake will not be serious enough to negate consent and the contract will have been formed (*Smith v Hughes* (1871) LR 6 QB 597).

Mistake as to subject matter of contract

In *Raffles v Wichelhaus* two parties tried to contract for the sale of a consignment of cotton. The cotton was due to be transported from Bombay on a ship called 'The Peerless'. However, two ships were arriving from Bombay called the 'The Peerless' and while the seller meant one of those ships, the buyer meant the other ship. The court held that no agreement had been reached because it was impossible to identify which ship the contract referred to – the terms were too ambiguous. Thus, there was no contract since the mistake had negated consent. From this case we can see that a mutual mistake will prevent the formation of the contract where the mistake or ambiguity is as to the subject matter of the contract. However, if the ambiguity or mistake is only about a secondary characteristic, then the contract will be valid.

Mistake as to secondary characteristic

In *Smith v Hughes* two parties contracted for the sale of some oats. The buyer meant to buy old oats, but in fact the oats were new oats. The buyer tried to argue that there was no contract on grounds of mistake, but the contract was simply for the sale of 'oats' and the court held that an agreement had been reached because the subject matter had been identified. Whether the oats were new or old was just a secondary characteristic, and the age of the oats did not form part of the subject matter of the contract. The court held that a mistake or ambiguity about a secondary characteristic (the age of the oats) did not affect the formation of the agreement.

In summary, no agreement will be formed if the parties were talking at cross-purposes and the mistake is fundamental and goes to the subject matter of the contract, preventing agreement. If the mistake is as to a secondary characteristic or quality, the contract is formed.

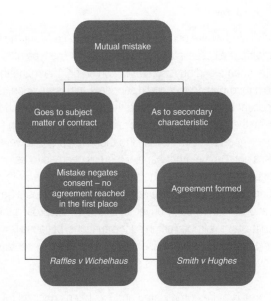

Unilateral mistake

Unilateral mistake occurs where just one of the parties makes a mistake and the other party to the contract takes advantage of that mistake – no agreement is reached. There will be no agreement where one party makes a mistake about a term of the contract, such as the price (*Hartog v Colin and Shield* [1939] 3 All ER 566). The law is more confusing where one party makes a mistake about the identity of the person they are contracting with; we will look at the cases on unilateral mistake as to identity below.

Unilateral mistake as to the terms of the contract (namely price)

In *Hartog v Colin and Shields* the parties contracted for the sale of some animal skins. When pricing up the skins, the seller had meant to sell them per piece, and the negotiations leading up to the contract had taken place on the basis that the price was per piece. However, the seller mistakenly made an offer to the buyer on a price based upon the weight of the skins (per pound). The buyer must have known about the mistake. The court ignored the written words of the contract here (which would usually represent the objective intention of the parties) and applied the subjective intention of the parties. The court held that no agreement had been reached because the buyer took advantage of the seller's mistake; the mistake negated consent. Usually, the objective intention of the parties is applied in order to protect the party relying on the words in the contract. However, in this case the court considered the subjective intention of the seller because the buyer deserved no protection since they were seeking to take advantage of the seller's mistake.

Unilateral mistake as to identity

The law is quite complicated where one party makes a mistake about the identity of the party they are contracting with. The cases in this area all deal with the type of situation where a rogue assumes another name and buys something on credit. The rogue then immediately sells the goods on to a third-party buyer and disappears. In this situation, the law must decide which of the two innocent parties (the seller and the third-party buyer) should suffer the loss. If the contract between the seller and the rogue is deemed to have been formed, then the third party can keep the goods (title has passed to the third party). However, in this situation, the original seller loses out. On the other hand, if there is deemed to be no contract between the seller and the rogue on the basis that the seller made a mistake as to rogue's identity, then title in the property did not pass to the rogue so the goods should be returned to seller. However, in this situation, the third-party buyer loses out. The approach taken by the courts in relation to the law on mistake is important in such situations, because is it not possible to avoid the contract under an alternative cause of action for misrepresentation since a third party gaining rights over the property acts as a bar to rescission.

The case law in this area is quite complicated and has been criticised for making artificial and illogical distinctions. The courts have drawn a distinction between face-to-face negotiations and negotiations at a distance. Where the parties have negotiated face-to-face, there is a contract because there is a presumption that the seller intended to deal with the person physically present in front of him (the rogue). Where the parties have negotiated at a distance (such as through the use of written forms), there is deemed to be no contract because the seller intended to deal with the person identified on the agreement (the assumed name).

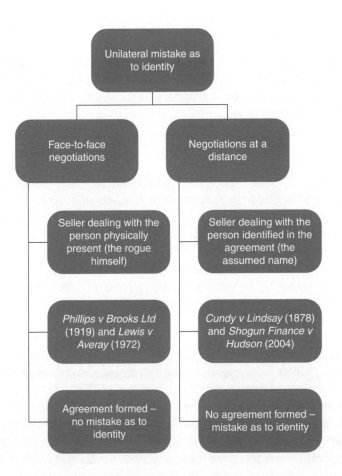

Face-to-face negotiations

In cases involving face-to-face negotiations, there is a contract between the seller and the person physically present in front of him (the rogue).

KEY CASE ANALYSIS: *Phillips v Brooks Ltd* **[1919] 2 KB 243**

Background

A jeweller sold a ring to a rogue who was posing as a wealthy and famous businessman called Sir George Bullough. The jeweller made checks to confirm that a person by that name did live at the address given, but did not carry out a check that the man in front of him was in fact Sir George Bullough. The rogue purported to pay by cheque, but the cheque bounced and the rogue could not be found. The ring had been sold on to a third-party buyer. The jeweller tried to argue that title in the ring remained with the jeweller because, due to the mistake, no contract had been formed.

Principle established

The court held that there was a contract because the jeweller had intended to deal with the person physically present in the shop (the rogue) despite the assumed name given. Thus, there was no mistake as to identity and the jeweller could not recover the ring from the third-party buyer.

Similarly, in the case of *Lewis v Averay* [1972] 1 QB 198, a rogue, who claimed to be a famous actor called Richard Greene, contracted to buy a car from the seller. The rogue produced a Pinewood Studios pass to prove his identity and on this basis he was allowed to drive away with a car in return for a cheque. He sold the car on to a third-party buyer and the cheque bounced. The court reached the same decision as in *Phillips v Brooks Ltd*, that the seller had been intending to deal with the person physically present in front of him (the rogue); thus, there was no mistake as to identity and the contract was formed. The seller could not recover the car since title in the car had passed to the third-party buyer.

Where checks are made as to the identity of the person, these checks could displace the presumption that the seller intends to deal with the rogue and so there will be no agreement on grounds of mistake, as in the case of *Ingram v Little* [1961] 1 QB 31. This case involved two sisters who were selling a car. They negotiated with a rogue who had provided the assumed name of Hutchinson. Having gone to the Post Office to check his name and address against an entry in a telephone directory, they accepted a cheque and the rogue took the car and sold it to a third-party buyer. The Court of Appeal held that the check carried out by the sisters meant that they had intended to deal with the assumed name, rather than the rogue who was physically present. This meant that there was no contract, and therefore the car still belonged to them. This decision is difficult to reconcile with both *Phillips v Brooks Ltd* and *Lewis v Averay*, and later cases have not succeeded in justifying the differences between the decisions, but instead the courts have stated simply that each cases rests on its own facts (see *Citibank NA v Brown Shipley & Co Ltd* [1991] 2 All ER 690).

Negotiations at a distance

Where the contract is negotiated at a distance and parties do not see each other, such as where the contract is negotiated in writing, then the seller is deemed to intend to deal with the name on paper (the assumed name). Thus, there is a mistake because the assumed name has not given their agreement, so the mistake negates the agreement.

KEY CASE ANALYSIS: *Cundy v Lindsay* (1878) 3 App Cas 459

Background

In this case, the rogue wrote to Lindsay ordering goods from him. The rogue had set up business in the name of Blenkarn, trading at 37 Wood Street. Lindsay knew of a firm called Blenkiron at 123 Wood Street. The rogue signed the letter to give the impression that the order had come from Blenkiron. As a result of the letter, Lindsay sent the goods to the rogue on credit and the rogue sold them on to a third-party buyer.

Principle established

The court held that Lindsay intended to deal with the name identified on paper (Blenkiron); Lindsay knew nothing of the rogue, thought nothing of the rogue and never intended to deal with the rogue. Therefore, there was a mistake as to identity because the real Blenkiron never gave their agreement to the contract. Thus, mistake as to identity prevented the formation of the contract and title to the goods remained with Lindsay.

In summary, with face-to-face negotiations the seller is deemed to intend to deal with the person physically present (the rogue), thus there is a contract and the third-party buyer receives good title to the goods. The opposite applies with negotiations at a distance, where the seller is deemed to intend to deal with the assumed name, thus there is no contract and the seller can recover the goods from the third-party buyer.

KEY CASE ANALYSIS: *Shogun Finance v Hudson* [2004] 1 AC 919

Background

This case presented difficulties for the courts because the contract was not entirely face-to-face, but neither was it entirely by correspondence. In fact, the negotiations took place via an intermediary (the car dealer). The rogue went to a car dealership and bought a car on a hire purchase agreement. The hire purchase agreement was with Shogun Finance, and the agreement was completed in writing via a hire purchase agreement form. However, the rogue signed the agreement using an assumed name, Mr Patel. He used a stolen driving licence as proof of identity.

Principle established

The case reached the House of Lords where, by a majority of 3:2, the House confirmed the existence of the distinction between face-to-face negotiations and negotiations at a distance. In this case, the House held that there were no face-to-face dealings between Shogun Finance and the rogue, so Shogun Finance could only intend to deal with the assumed name, Mr Patel. Thus, the House adopted the approach taken for negotiations at a distance and there was no contract. Therefore, title in the car remained with Shogun Finance.

This decision has been the subject of much academic criticism. The distinction between face-to-face negotiations and negotiations at a distance seems to be an artificial and illogical one, and is complicated. It is difficult to see how this distinction can be maintained in light of increasing developments in modern-day technology. For instance, how are negotiations via video conferencing or via internet calls using Skype to be treated?

On-the-spot question

Fred places an advert on a website advertising for sale rare paintings by a famous Dutch expressionist. He is contacted via text message by a rogue who states that he is interested in purchasing the paintings. Fred and the rogue agree to a virtual meeting using an internet video conferencing application. At the online meeting, the rogue introduces himself as 'Victor Gorky', a Russian art dealer. Fred agrees to sell the paintings to the rogue on credit.

Is there a valid contract for sale here?

COMMON MISTAKE

Common mistake is different to communication mistake. Common mistake occurs where the parties have reached an agreement, but they have made a fundamental mistake at the time of or before the formation of the contract that goes to the very root of the contract, so that the problem makes performance of the contract impossible or very different to what was intended. Where there is common mistake, the contract will be void for mistake.

Fundamental mistake

The simplest example of common mistake is where the subject matter of the contract does not actually exist. The case of *Couturier v Hastie* (1856) 5 HL 673 concerned a contract for the sale of corn, which was believed to be on a ship on its way to the UK. However, before that contract had been formed, the master of the ship sold the corn because it had deteriorated so much. Neither party knew at the time of contracting that the master of the ship had sold the corn. The House of Lords held that the contract for the sale of the corn was void because performance of the contract was impossible – there was a total lack of consideration as the corn did not exist at the time of contracting. It is worth noting here that if the corn had existed at the time of contracting, but was later disposed of, then this case would have fallen within the topic of frustration. Frustration occurs where an event takes place after the formation of the contract and renders performance impossible (see Chapter 9). In such a situation, the contract is discharged (rather than being held to be void). However, mistake occurs where the mistake has been in existence from the outset, making the contract impossible to perform.

Griffin v Brymer (1903) 19 TLR 434 is one of the Coronation cases. This case concerned the Coronation procession for King Edward VII. The contract was a contract for the hire of a room to view the Coronation procession. However, the King was taken ill and the procession was cancelled. The Coronation was actually cancelled before the parties entered into a contract, and thus this was a mistake case, rather than a frustration case. However, at the time that the parties formed the agreement, neither party knew that the procession had been cancelled. Therefore, the parties reached their agreement under the mistaken belief there would be a Coronation, but the Coronation had already been cancelled. In light of this, the contract was held to be void for mistake.

Common mistake also applies where the parties make a mistake about who has good title to property. For instance, if I try to buy something that already belongs to me, and neither I nor the seller know that I already have title to the property, this would constitute a common mistake. The contract for sale would be void for mistake. This is essentially what happened in *Cooper v Phibbs* (1867) LR 2 HL 149. The plaintiff agreed to lease a fishery, but neither Cooper nor the seller knew that Cooper already had the right to enjoy the fishery under his existing tenancy agreement, and hence there had been no need for any additional lease. The court held that performance of this contract was impossible because Cooper had been trying to acquire a right that he already had. Thus, the lease agreement was void for mistake.

Mistake as to essential quality

However, common mistake does not apply where the mistake is not fundamental (does not go to the root or subject matter of the contract), and instead relates to some characteristic or quality of the contract.

KEY CASE ANALYSIS: *Bell v Lever Bros Ltd* [1932] AC 161, HL

Background

This is the leading case on this point. In this case, Lever Bros agreed to pay significant redundancy packages to two directors of a subsidiary company; the payment was made as compensation for the termination of their employment contracts. However, the two directors had previously breached their contracts of employment by engaging in some inappropriate business conduct. As such, the directors could actually have been dismissed without the redundancy payment being made, although neither the directors nor Lever Bros were aware of this at the time of agreeing to a redundancy payment. Lever Bros asked the court to rule that the redundancy agreements were void for mistake so that the money paid could be returned to Lever Bros.

Principle established

By a 3:2 majority, the House of Lords held that the redundancy agreement was valid since there had been no mistake as to the subject matter of the agreement, namely the contract of employment. Irrespective of the amount of money paid in compensation, the subject matter of the contract was the same; it was still a contract about employment, it was not essentially different. The House held that the mistake had been made only as to the amount of money negotiated as redundancy pay, and that this was merely an attribute or characteristic of the contract, but did not make the contract essentially different. Thus, the contract was not void for mistake. Lord Atkin stated that a contract would only be void for mistake if the parties' mistake went to the essence of the contract, if '[t]he existence of some quality which makes the thing without that quality essentially different from the thing it was believed to be'.

Lord Atkin provided two examples relating to the sale of horses.

Example 1

In the first example, Lord Atkin stated that where you contract to buy a horse, which is believed to be sound, but the horse actually turns out to be unsound, the contract is not void for mistake. A horse is still a horse, and whether the horse is sound is a question of quality, but is not of fundamental importance to the contract, thus the contract is not essentially different.

Example 2

In his second example, Lord Atkin stated that where you contract to buy a racehorse, but the horse you get actually turns out to be a carthorse, then the contract is void for mistake. This would make the contract essentially different from what it was meant to be because a racehorse is essentially different from a carthorse.

Thus, the doctrine of mistake was applied very narrowly in order that a person may not simply use mistake to escape from a bad bargain. However, this case has been heavily criticised by leading academics. In an article called 'Contracts – mistake, frustration and implied terms' [1994] LQR 400, Professor JC Smith took the view that *Bell v Lever Bros Ltd* was wrongly decided. He stated that if the mistake as to the level of compensation in this contract was not fundamental enough, then no mistake would ever be fundamental enough: 'it is impossible to envisage a mistake as to quality which is more fundamental than that' (at p412).

On-the-spot question

 When is a contract void for common mistake? Can the decision in *Bell v Lever Bros Ltd* be justified?

Denning LJ took the opportunity to explore common mistake in the case of *Leaf v International Galleries* [1950] 2 KB 86. This case involved the sale of a painting. The buyer (Leaf) and the seller (International Galleries) both mistakenly believed that a painting was an old Master by Constable of Salisbury Cathedral. At the time of contracting, both parties made the mistake. Five years later, when Leaf tried to sell the painting, he discovered that the painting was in fact a fake. Leaf tried to sue International Galleries for misrepresentation, but the lapse of time since the sale constituted a bar to rescission. Denning LJ made an *obiter* statement regarding common mistake, stating that the mistake as to quality (as to the identity of the painter) would not have been sufficient to render the contract void for mistake,

> There was a mistake about the quality of the subject-matter, because both parties believed the picture to be a Constable; and that mistake was in one sense essential or fundamental. But such a mistake does not avoid the contract: there was no mistake at all about the subject-matter of the sale. It was a specific picture, 'Salisbury Cathedral'. The parties were agreed in the same terms on the same subject-matter, and that is sufficient to make a contract.

The opinion of Denning LJ was echoed by Lord Evershed MR:

> What he contracted to buy and what he bought was a specific chattel, namely, an oil painting of Salisbury Cathedral; but he bought it on the faith of a representation, innocently made, that it had been painted by John Constable. It turns out, as the evidence now stands . . ., that it was not so painted. Nevertheless it remains true to say that the plaintiff still has the article which he contracted to buy. The difference is no doubt considerable, but it is, as Denning LJ has observed, a difference in quality and in value rather than in the substance of the thing itself.

Thus, the contract could not be void for mistake.

KEY CASE ANALYSIS: *Great Peace Shipping Ltd v Tsavliris (International) Ltd* [2002] EWCA Civ 1407

Background

The defendant salvage company was asked to assist a ship that had got into trouble in the South Indian Ocean. The defendants contacted the claimants, The Great Peace, who both parties thought was 35 miles away from the troubled ship, in order to hire the Great Peace for five days as part of the salvage operation. It later transpired that actually the Great Peace was 410 miles away from the troubled ship, and the defendants sought to cancel the contract with the Great Peace on the grounds of common mistake.

Principle established

The Court of Appeal held that the contract for hire was valid because the mistake did not go to the root of the contract. The location of the vessel was merely a characteristic of the contract and was not fundamental to it, thus the service to be provided would not be essentially different to that which the parties had agreed.

The Court of Appeal followed the narrow approach taken by the House of Lords in *Bell v Lever Bros Ltd* and held that common mistake will render a contract void if the following elements are present:

- there must be a common assumption as to the existence of a state of affairs;
- there must be no warranty by either party that that state of affairs exists;
- the non-existence of the state of affairs must not be attributable to the fault of either party;

- the non-existence of the state of affairs must render performance of the contract impossible; and
- the state of affairs may be the existence, or a vital attribute, of the consideration to be provided or circumstances that must subsist if performance of the contractual adventure is to be possible.

Rescission in equity for common mistake

On-the-spot question

 If the law will only allow a party to escape from a contract under the doctrine of mistake in very rare circumstances, do you think that equity could be of any assistance?

In the Court of Appeal in *Solle v Butcher* [1950] 1 KB 671, Denning LJ sought to avoid the harsh operation of the doctrine of mistake and held that although not void in law, a contract was voidable in equity due to the parties' fundamental mistake. However, in *Great Peace Shipping Ltd v Tsavliris (International) Ltd*, the Court of Appeal disapproved of Denning LJ's *obiter* comments in *Solle v Butcher* on the basis that it could not be reconciled with *Bell v Lever Bros Ltd* and because the courts should not protect parties against extremely bad bargains.

SUMMARY

- Communication mistake is where the parties fail to reach an agreement and this renders the contract void. There are two types of communication mistake: mutual mistake where the parties negotiate at cross-purposes, and unilateral mistake where one party takes advantage of the other's mistake.
- Mutual mistake will only render a contract void where the mistake is fundamental (such as a mistake as to the subject matter of the contract) and not merely about a secondary characteristic.
- Where there is a mistake as to identity and the parties have negotiated face-to-face, there is a contract because there is a presumption that the seller intended to deal with the person physically present in front of him (the rogue). Where the parties have negotiated at a distance, there is deemed to be no contract

because the seller intended to deal with the person identified on the agreement (the assumed name).

- Common mistake occurs where the parties have reached an agreement, but they have made a fundamental mistake that goes to the root of the contract, rendering performance of the contract impossible or very different to what was intended. There is no common mistake where the mistake is merely as to an essential quality or characteristic that is not fundamental.

FURTHER READING

Beatson J, Burrows A and Cartwright J, *Anson's Law of Contract*, 29th edn (Oxford University Press, 2010) (Chapter 8) – This textbook provides a detailed analysis of the law relating to mistake.

MacMillan C, 'Rogues, Swindlers and Cheats: The Development of Mistake of identity in English Contract Law' (2005) 64 CLJ 711 – This article provides a detailed analysis of the development of the doctrine of mistake as to identity.

Poole J, *Textbook on Contract Law*, 10th edn (2010), OUP (Chapters 3 and 13) – This textbook provides an excellent explanation of the law on mistake.

Smith JC, 'Contracts – mistake, frustration and implied terms' [1994] LQR 400 – This article provides an excellent commentary on the case of *Bell v Lever Bros Ltd*.

Thomas S, 'Mistake of identity: a comparative analysis' (2008) LMCLQ 188 – This article explores the decision in *Shogun Finance v Hudson* and contrasts English law with the United States Uniform Commercial Code.

COMPANION WEBSITE

An online glossary compiled by the authors is available on the companion website: www.routledge.com/cw/beginningthelaw

Chapter 7
Duress, undue influence and illegality

LEARNING OUTCOMES

After reading this chapter, you should be able to:

- Appreciate the difference between duress and undue influence
- Demonstrate knowledge of the law relating to duress
- Understand the requirements for economic duress
- Differentiate between a legitimate and an illegitimate commercial pressure
- Explain what is meant by actual undue influence and presumed undue influence

INTRODUCTION

This chapter will look at duress, undue influence and illegality. Duress and undue influence are factors that will vitiate a contract (i.e. potentially bring the contract to an end; if a contract is illegal then the courts will not generally enforce the contract).

Key Definitions

Duress – The coercion of a contracting party's consent that renders the contract voidable. There can be physical duress where the coercion is unlawful or economic duress where it is illegitimate pressure.

Undue influence – An equitable doctrine that renders a contract voidable where one party unfairly exploits their relationship with the other contracting party in order to gain their consent.

Illegality – A court will refuse to enforce a contract where it is illegal under statute or the common law.

DURESS

Duress is a vitiating factor that will make a contract voidable. Whether the contract is set aside will be at the discretion of the court. A party having entered into a contract may seek at a later date to argue that the court should not be valid, as their free will has been overcome by unlawful pressure.

Physical duress

Traditionally, only physical duress was accepted as a vitiating factor. There needed to be unlawful pressure that constituted a physical threat towards the claimant.

KEY CASE ANALYSIS: *Barton v Armstrong* [1976] AC 104

Background

The claimant and the defendant owned shares in a company. The defendant had made threats to the claimant's life in order to make the claimant purchase the respondent's shares. These threats included, 'The city is not as safe as you may think between office and home. You will see what I can do against you and you will regret the day when you decided not to work with me'.

Principle established

The majority of the Privy Council held that the claimant's decision to purchase the shares had been made under duress and the contract was void.

Lord Cross was clear that:

- the burden of proof was on the defendant to prove that the threats had not contributed to the claimant's decision to buy the shares;
- there needed to be unlawful pressure;
- it was irrelevant that there might have been other considerations for purchasing the shares (i.e. commercial considerations).

Economic duress

The ability to set aside a contract for economic duress was accepted in *Occidental Worldwide Investment Corp v Skibs A/S Avanti (The Siboen and The Sibotre)* [1976] 1 Lloyd's Rep 293. Although the party seeking to set aside the contract was under pressure, the pressure did not amount to coercion. In *Pao On v Lau Yiu Long* [1980] AC 614, the Privy Council accepted *obiter* that economic duress could be relied upon to set aside a contract. On behalf of the Privy Council, Lord Scarman stated that in order for economic duress to 'render a contract voidable . . . it must amount to a coercion of will, which vitiates consent. It must be shown that the payment made or the contract entered into was not a voluntary act'. Crucially, His Lordship stated that there needs to be a coercion of will that prevents the claimant from having truly consented to entering into the contract.

KEY CASE ANALYSIS: *Universe Tankships Inc of Monrovia v International Transport Workers Federation (The Universe Sentinel)* [1983] 1 AC 366

Background

The defendant trade union told the dock workers at a harbour to refuse to operate tugs to allow the release of the vessel, *The Universe Sentinel*, which was docked in the harbour. In a dispute over the pay that had been given to the crew of the vessel, the trade union demanded that the plaintiffs pay the crew the money owed to them in pay and an additional sum of $6,480 in order to secure the release of the vessel. The plaintiffs paid all sums, and after the release of the vessel sued to recover the additional sum of $6,480.

Principle established

The House of Lords accepted that the plaintiff had made payments to the defendant under economic duress and the money could be recovered by the plaintiffs. Lord Diplock provided valuable guidance on economic duress:

> The rationale is that his apparent consent was induced by pressure exercised upon him by [the] other party which the law does not regard as legitimate, with the consequence that the consent is treated in law as revocable unless approbated either expressly or by implication after the illegitimate pressure has ceased to operate on his mind . . .
>
> Commercial pressure, in some degree, exists wherever one party to a commercial transaction is in a stronger bargaining position than the other party. It is not, however, in my view, necessary, nor would it be appropriate in the instant appeal, to enter into the general question of the kinds of circumstances, if any, in which commercial pressure, even though it amounts to a coercion of the will of a party in the weaker bargaining position, may be treated as legitimate and, accordingly, as not giving rise to any legal right of redress.

Lord Diplock is quite clear in his judgment that there needs to be illegitimate pressure that overcomes the claimant's consent at the time he enters into the contract. It is not a question of the claimant not understanding the terms of the contract. The commercial pressure may coerce the weaker contracting party but it may be regarded as legitimate. However, on the facts, the economic pressure concerned industrial relations and was considered an illegitimate commercial pressure. It is crucial that the pressure must be a significant cause of the party entering into the contract.

It is interesting to look at what type of commercial pressure is considered illegitimate by the courts. A good example is *Atlas Express Ltd v Kafco (Importers and Distributors) Ltd* [1989] QB 833. Here there was a contract for the delivery of goods. The claimants had agreed to deliver goods to Woolworths on behalf of the defendants. The claimant forced the defendant to renegotiate the contractual delivery price by threatening to breach the contract. The defendant acceded to the claimant's demands because they were in a difficult position, having secured a lucrative contract with a large retailer, Woolworths, which they needed to fulfil, and they doubted their ability to find an alternative party to deliver the goods. The court held that the defendant's consent was vitiated by economic duress because the defendants knew they had no alternative. As Tucker J stated, 'I accept the evidence of the Woolworths manager, Mr Graham, that if the defendants had told them that they could not supply the goods, Woolworths would have sued them for loss of profit and would have ceased trading with them. I find that this was well-known to the defendants' directors'. Tucker J found that the consent was induced by illegitimate pressure.

On-the-spot question

 In *Atlas Express Ltd*, why did the court find that there was illegitimate pressure?

Dyson J restated the requirements for economic duress in *DSND Subsea Ltd v Petroleum Geo Services ASA* [2000] BLR 530. His Lordship stated that there were three requirements to illegitimate pressure: the pressure has to result in the victim having no other practical choice, the pressure has to be illegitimate, and the pressure must be a significant cause in the victim entering into the contract.

It is clear that the party claiming that there has been economic duress must protest that their consent was obtained by a coercion of their will. According to Dyson J in *DSND Subsea Ltd*, 'whether there has been an actual or threatened breach of contract; whether the person allegedly exerting the pressure has acted in good or bad faith; whether the victim had any realistic practical alternative but to submit to the pressure; whether the victim protested at the time; and whether he affirmed and sought to rely on the contract' should be taken into consideration by the courts in determining if there had been economic duress.

- 'There must be pressure:

- The practical effect of which is that there is compulsion on, or a lack of practical choice for the victim,

- that is illegitimate, and

- that is a significant cause inducing the claimant to enter into the contract.'

Link with consideration

We have seen how economic duress can be used as a defence where the defendant is being sued for the contract price. Promises to pay more in return for the same service were not considered enforceable for lack of new consideration (see Chapter 3 and *Stilk v Myrick*). However, despite the concept of practical benefit, a promise to pay more will be unenforceable where the renegotiated price has been obtained by economic duress.

On-the-spot question

Andy owns Little Hampstead House and has hired Historic Actors Ltd (HAL) to recreate life in the sixteenth century. Andy has advertised the historical re-enactment during the August bank holiday and is expecting a large number of visitors. HAL informs him three days before the day it is due to provide the actors that unless Andy pays £500 more, they will not be able to provide the actors. Reluctantly, Andy agrees and pays the £500. Three months later, when HAL submits its invoice, Andy decides not to pay it. HAL is now suing Andy for breach of contract.

Advise Andy.

UNDUE INFLUENCE

The doctrine of undue influence is an equitable doctrine that enables a court to set aside a contract (i.e. it renders the contract voidable). Undue influence requires that there is a relationship between the parties that one party has exploited to their benefit. As Lord Hoffmann stated in *R v Attorney General of England and Wales* [2003] UKPC 22:

... undue influence is based upon the principle that a transaction to which consent has been obtained by unacceptable means should not be allowed to stand. Undue influence has concentrated in particular upon the unfair exploitation by one party of a relationship which gives him ascendancy or influence over the other.

In *Barclays Bank v O'Brien* [1993] 4 All ER 417, Lord Browne-Wilkinson held that undue influence could be classified into different types of undue influence (approving the classifications suggested in *Bank of Credit and Commerce International SA v Aboody* [1990] 1 QB 923). Accordingly, there are two types of undue influence:

- Actual undue influence (Class 1).
- Presumed undue influence (Class 2).

Actual undue influence

Actual undue influence arises where undue influence is actually exerted on one party such that the free will of that party in deciding to enter into the contract is compromised. This type of undue influence does not require there to be a special relationship of trust and confidence between the parties.

Presumed undue influence

Presumed undue influence arises where undue influence is presumed to have been exerted because of the relationship between the parties. There must be a special relationship of trust and confidence between the parties which has been exploited by one party. In *Barclays Bank v O'Brien*, this category of presumed undue influence was further broken down according to the types of relationship between the parties:

- Class 2A – encompassed certain relationships where the presumption of undue influence was automatic in law.
- Class 2B – applied to relationships where there was no automatic presumption of undue influence, but on the facts of the case one party placed particular trust and confidence in the other party.

However, the House of Lords has since had an opportunity to revisit the doctrine of undue influence and the leading case on undue influence is now *Royal Bank of Scotland v Etridge (No 2)* [2001] 4 All ER 449.

Class 2A – Automatic presumption of influence

In *Etridge (No 2)*, the House of Lords held that in class 2A cases, the claimant did not need to prove that he placed trust and confidence in the other party, but he merely needs to prove the existence of a special relationship that falls under class 2A. Relationships that fall under class 2A include solicitor–client, doctor–patient, parent–child and trustee–beneficiary. In such cases, there is an automatic presumption that some pressure or influence has been exerted on the party, but there is no presumption that the pressure or influence is undue.

Class 2B – Relationships of trust and confidence

In cases where there is no automatic presumption of influence under class 2A, there may still be a relationship of trust and confidence from which influence can be inferred. The nature of the relationship between the parties will need to be explored and the claimant will need to prove that he placed trust and confidence in the other party. This class applies to relationships such as husband and wife.

Does it call for explanation?

Once influence is established, the court must go on to consider whether the transaction is one that cannot be reasonably accounted for on the grounds of friendship or some other ordinary motive and calls for an explanation. The rationale for this requirement is 'to prevent the presumption applying to obviously innocuous transactions between those in a relationship of trust and confidence, such as a moderate gift as a Christmas present by a child to a parent, an agreement by a client to pay the reasonable fees to a solicitor, or a moderate bequest to one's doctor' (Beatson J *et al, Anson's Law of Contract* (29th edn, OUP, 2010) at p365). According to *Etridge (No 2)*, there is no longer a need to demonstrate a 'manifest disadvantage' to the party placing confidence in the other.

Guidelines from *Etridge (No 2)*

KEY CASE ANALYSIS: *Royal Bank of Scotland v Etridge (No 2)* [2001] 4 All ER 449

Background

Etridge (No 2) involved a number of cases with similar facts in which a husband took out a business loan that he secured against the jointly owned matrimonial home, his wife having agreed to secure the loan against their home. In each case, the wife later claimed that she agreed under the undue influence of her husband. The cases involved a third party, namely a bank, who was acting on behalf of the husband. Where the transaction is obviously not of any benefit to the wife, the bank is put on inquiry and would be fixed with constructive notice of undue influence unless it takes reasonable steps to ensure that the wife has entered into the contract of her own free will.

Principle established

The House of Lords provided that the wife should have the opportunity to seek independent legal advice and she should have a separate meeting with her solicitor in private. It is for the bank to provide the wife's solicitor with the necessary financial information relating to the transaction. Her solicitor should write to the bank to confirm that the risks and implications of the transaction have been explained to the wife.

If the solicitor does not confirm this to the bank directly, the bank will not avoid being fixed with constructive notice of undue influence; it is not enough that the bank is simply aware that the wife has instructed her own solicitor: *First National Bank v Achampong* (2003) EWCA Civ 487.

On-the-spot question

 Explain the difference between actual and presumed undue influence.

ILLEGALITY

Contracts that are illegal either because of statute or common law will not be enforced by the courts. At common law the courts will not enforce a contract that they consider to go against public policy. Neither will the courts enforce a contract to break the law or to trade with the enemy.

SUMMARY

- Duress renders a contract voidable and may be physical duress or economic duress (based on illegitimate pressure). For economic duress, the courts are aware that a commercial party is expected to exploit their stronger position, therefore the pressure applied must be illegitimate before the courts will hold that duress is present.

- Undue influence is an equitable doctrine that renders a contract voidable where one party unfairly exploits their relationship with the other contracting party in order to gain their consent. The courts will distinguish between actual and presumed undue influence.
- A court will refuse to enforce a contract where it is illegal under statute or the common law.

FURTHER READING

Bigwood R, 'Undue influence in the House of Lords: principles and proof' [2002] 65(3) MLR 435 – This article explores the House of Lords' decision in *Etridge (No 2)*.

Boon A and Phang L, 'Whiter economic duress? Reflections on two recent cases' [1990] 53(1) MLR 107 – This article looks at the decision in *Atlas Express Ltd*.

Lal H, 'Commercial exploitation in construction contracts: the role of economic duress and unjust enrichment' [2005] 21(8) Const LJ 590 – This article looks at the use of pressure in contracts.

Stone R, *The Modern Law of Contract*, 9th edn (Routledge, 2011) – Refer to this textbook for a more advanced exploration of the issues raised in this chapter.

Wong S, 'Revisiting Barclays v O'Brien and independent legal advice for vulnerable sureties' [2002] JBL 439 – This article considers the scope and application of the *O'Brien* principle.

COMPANION WEBSITE

An online glossary compiled by the authors is available on the companion website: www.routledge.com/cw/beginningthelaw

Chapter 8
Privity of contract

LEARNING OUTCOMES

After reading this chapter, you should be able to:

- Understand the common law doctrine of privity
- Appreciate the development of the key common law and statutory exceptions
- Be able to demonstrate an understanding of why the Contracts (Rights of Third Parties) Act 1999 was introduced
- Conclude whether a third party can ever enforce a term in a contract

INTRODUCTION

Only parties to a contract can enforce the contract in a court of law. The common law doctrine of privity of contract prevents third parties from being able to enforce terms in the contract (i.e. to sue) and from incurring liability. This rule is the general rule and, as we shall see, there are a number of common law and statutory exceptions. These exceptions shall be discussed below.

GENERAL RULE

As a general rule, contracts can only be enforced by a party to the contract. Third parties are unable to enforce a contract unless they themselves have acquired a right to enforce it by providing consideration.

KEY CASE ANALYSIS: *Dunlop Pneumatic Tyre Co Ltd v Selfridge & Co Ltd* [1915] AC 847

Background

In this case Dunlop had sold tyres to Dew and the parties had agreed in their contract that the tyres should not be sold for less than the minimum list price. Dew then resold the tyres to Selfridge & Co, who in turn sold the tyres for less than the price

---

previously specified by Dunlop. Dunlop then sought to enforce this term against Selfridge & Co. The issue was whether Dunlop could sue Selfridge & Co for breach of contract.

Principle established

The House of Lords refused to allow Dunlop to enforce a contract against Selfridge & Co, as there was no privity of contract between them. Lord Haldane LC stated:

> My Lords, in the law of England certain principles are fundamental. One is that only a person who is a party to a contract can sue on it. Our law knows nothing of a *jus quaesitum tertio* arising by way of contract. Such a right may be conferred by way of property, as, for example, under a trust, but it cannot be conferred on a stranger to a contract as a right to enforce the contract *in personam*.

In *Tweddle v Atkinson* (1861) 1 Best and Smith 393, the court ruled that a third party could not enforce a contract, even if that contract conferred a benefit on the third party. Two fathers, upon the marriage of their children, to each other, both promised verbally to each give money to the husband. One of the fathers died and his executor refused to pay the promised amount to the husband. The husband was unable to enforce the contract because he was not a party to it. In *Beswick v Beswick* [1968] AC 58 the issue was whether a widow could enforce a contract made between her late husband and her nephew. Her husband had sold his business to his nephew. Their contract provided for the payment of £5 a week to his wife upon his death. Upon the death of her husband, the nephew paid one instalment of £5, but then ceased all payments. The wife sued but the House of Lords held that in her personal capacity she was unable to enforce the contract, as she had not been privy to the contract. However, she could enforce the contract in the capacity of the administrator of her late husband's estate. The House of Lords held that she was entitled under s 56 Law of Property Act 1925 to demand the payment by way of specific performance.

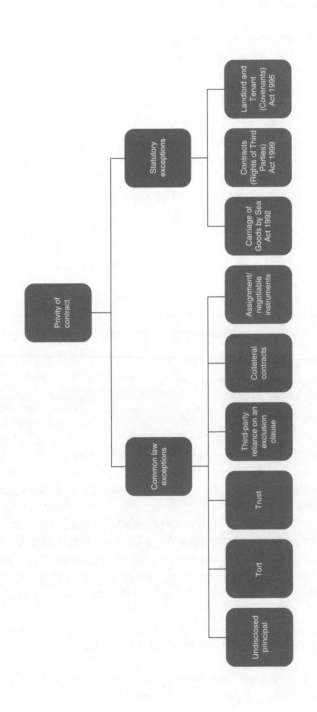

COMMON LAW EXCEPTIONS

There are a number of important common law exceptions to the doctrine of privity of contract. We will consider these exceptions in turn.

Tort

Liability in tort does not depend on a contract between the parties. Traditionally, there was a great reluctance to extend liability in tort as there was a belief that liability should be limited to the parties' contractual obligations. The key case that developed the modern tort of negligence was *Donoghue v Stevenson* [1932] AC 562. Here, the House of Lords held that a duty of care could be owed in specific circumstances to anyone, regardless of whether there was an existing contractual relationship. In *Donoghue v Stevenson*, the claimant's friend had purchased ginger beer (which turned out to contain a decomposed snail) from a cafe owner. The claimant drank the ginger beer and had become ill after discovering a decomposed snail. The claimant could not sue the café owner as she was not privy to the contract for sale of the ginger beer. However, the House of Lords held that a duty of care was owed by the manufacturer of the ginger beer to Miss Donoghue. Therefore she was able to sue the manufacturer despite not being privy to a contract with the manufacturer.

Collateral contracts

It is possible for a third party to enforce a contract where they can argue that there is a collateral contract. In *Shanklin Pier Ltd v Detel Products Ltd* [1951] 2 KB 854 the claimant, who was the owner of a pier, agreed with the defendants, who were the manufacturers of paint, that the contractors who would paint the pier would use their product. The defendants had informed the claimant that the paint would have a lifetime of between seven to ten years. As instructed, the contractors entered into a contract with the defendant. The claimant was not privy to that contract. The paint turned out to be unsatisfactory and lasted only three months. The claimants were able to sue the defendants because the court held that there was a collateral contract between them, based upon their warranty that the paint would be suitable for the job. The claimant had provided consideration for this warranty by requiring the contractors to use that particular paint.

Third-party reliance on an exclusion clause

The House of Lords in *Scruttons Ltd v Midland Silicones Ltd* [1962] AC 446 ruled that a stevedore could not rely on a limitation clause contained in a contract between a carrier and a shipper. The carrier (the owner of the ship) and the shipper (the person shipping the goods) had contracted for the carriage of goods by sea. The Bill of Lading evidenced the terms of their contract and contained a limitation clause. The stevedore had contracted with the carrier to load the goods. The stevedore damaged the goods and attempted to rely on the limitation clause to limit liability. The House of Lords ruled that the stevedore was not privy to the original contract and therefore could not rely on the clause. This was because neither party was acting as an agent for the stevedore. Lord Denning dissented and argued that it was wrong that the shipper could sue the stevedore in negligence and avoid the limitations imposed on the amount he could have recovered from the carrier. However, the Privy Council held in *New Zealand Shipping Co Ltd v AM Satterthwaite & Co Ltd, The Eurymedon* [1975] AC 154 that a third party could enforce an exclusion clause where they were being sued by the shipper for negligence. This was because in this case, although the stevedore (independent contractor) was not privy to the carriage, the contract specifically contained a clause that said any independent contractor would be protected by the exclusion clause. The carrier was held to be acting as an agent for the stevedore. The Privy Council held that the shipper in the contract with the carrier was making a unilateral offer, which, once the stevedore had accepted via their performance, would entitle them to rely on the exclusion clause. The stevedore had provided sufficient consideration to enforce the promise.

On-the-spot question

In common law, can a third party ever rely on an exclusion clause?

Trusts

Trusts are another exception to the doctrine of privity of contract. If a person wishes to establish a trust either in their own lifetime or upon their death, they can create a trust and transfer property to a trustee. The trustee will own the legal title to the property, but will hold this on trust for the beneficiary (i.e. the person whom the trust intends to benefit). Thus, the trustee is able to enforce a contract made between the person who established the trust and the other party to a contract.

The undisclosed principal

An agent will enter into contracts with customers on behalf of a principal. Where the customer knows that the agent is acting for a principal, then the contract will be between the customer and the principal. An example of this is a website that sells tickets on behalf of West End theatres, such as lastminute.com. The contract is between the customer and the theatre (the principal), not between the customer and the website (the agent). However, if the customer does not know that there is a principal, then the contract will initially be between the agent and the customer. Controversially, the principal, despite not being privy to the contract, is able to intervene and enforce the contract himself. This was held to be an anomaly in *Keighley, Maxsted & Co v Durant* [1901] AC 240, and Sir Frederick Pollock was critical that it was inconsistent with privity of contract ([1887] 3 LQR 358). You will learn more about this should you study commercial law.

Assignment and negotiable instruments

Where two parties contract, one of the parties can assign their rights under a contract to a third party. This allows the third party to enforce the right of repayment of a debt against one of the original parties to a contract. Negotiable instruments (such as a cheque) are a way of transferring the contractual right of repayment of a debt to a third party.

On-the-spot question

? Mohamed has asked Boris to act as his agent and to enter into contracts on his behalf. Boris contracts to purchase a car from Pauline, without disclosing that he is acting as an agent. Pauline later finds out that Boris is only an agent and refuses to sell the car to Mohamed.

Can Mohamed enforce the contract against Pauline?

STATUTORY EXCEPTIONS

We will now look at some important statutory exceptions to the doctrine of privity of contract.

Contracts (Rights of Third Parties) Act 1999

The Contracts (Rights of Third Parties) Act 1999 ['C(RTP)A'] is an important statutory exception to the common law doctrine of privity of contract. The C(RPT)A does not permit a third party to be treated as a party to a contract (s 7(4)); however, the third party can enforce a contract.

Section 1(1) permits a third party to enforce a term in a contract in his own right, if the contract confers an express right to do this, or the term purports to confer a benefit on the third party. Section 1(2) outlines the circumstances when the contract will purport to confer a benefit on the third party. These are that the 'third party must be expressly identified in the contract by name, as a member of a class or as answering a particular description but need not be in existence when the contract is entered into'. Under subsection (5) the third party will have the same remedy for breach of that term as if he himself was a party to the contract.

It is important to note that the C(RPT)A is aimed at conferring a benefit and not a burden on third parties. The person who makes the promise that the third party wishes to enforce will have the same defences available, if it was the other party who was seeking to enforce the term (s 3). The C(RPT)A can also be expressly excluded in a contract (s 2(3)).

The Law Commission provided the impetus for reforming the common law doctrine of privity. The Law Commission published *Privity of Contract: Contracts for the Benefit of Third Parties* (Law Com No 242, 1996) and provided a draft Bill that was adopted by Parliament.

It should be remembered that the C(RPT)A, whilst being an important statutory exception, does not abolish the doctrine of privity of contract. The doctrine remains the general law, and it is important to appreciate that the C(RPT)A does not impact on some of the other existing exceptions.

Commenting on the effect of the C(RPT)A, Catharine MacMillan stated that 'The Act therefore gives a third party to a contract the right to enforce a term of that contract where the contracting parties intend to give the third party such a right . . . [Another reason for reform] was to overcome the injustice of the privity rule to the third party. A contract between A and B to confer a benefit upon C creates reasonable expectations on the part of C that he will have the right to enforce the contract . . . Where such a reasonable expectation has been created, it is not just for the law to deny C any benefit' (MacMillan [2000] MLR 721).

On-the-spot question

 How would you summarise the impact of the Contracts (Rights of Third Parties) Act 1999 on the common law doctrine of privity of contract?

Landlord and Tenant (Covenants) Act 1995

Another statutory exception to the doctrine of privity is the Landlord and Tenant (Covenants) Act 1995, which permits covenants in a lease between the landlord and tenant to be enforced by subsequent successor landlords and tenants. This has simplified the existing difficulties in enforcing covenants.

Carriage of Goods by Sea Act 1992

The Carriage of Goods by Sea Act 1992 also provides a statutory exception to the doctrine of privity. Section 2 of this Act permits the lawful holder of a bill of lading to have the right to sue the carrier under the original contract. This is an important exception that permits the owner of goods to enforce the contract made between the carrier (shipping company) and the shipper (the person shipping the goods), which will be vital if the goods are lost or damaged by the carrier.

SUMMARY

- Only parties to a contract can enforce the contract in a court of law. The doctrine of privity of contract prevents third parties from being able to sue on a contract and from being sued on a contract.
- There are a number of common law and statutory exceptions to the doctrine of privity, the most important of which is the Contracts (Rights of Third Parties) Act 1999.

FURTHER READING

Beatson J, Burrows A and Cartwright J, *Anson's Law of Contract*, 29th edn (Oxford University Press, 2010) – A comprehensive textbook that looks at this area in considerable detail.

Cheng-Han T, 'Undisclosed principals and contract' [2004] 120 *Law Quarterly Review* 480 – This article explores the use of undisclosed principal and defends this area of the law.

Law Commission, *Privity of Contract: Contracts for the Benefit of Third Parties* (Law Com No 242, 1996) – A thorough discussion on the law and the need for reform.

MacMillan C, 'A Birthday Present for Lord Denning: The Contracts (Rights of Third Parties) Act 1999' [2000] 63 *The Modern Law Review* 721 – A good article on the C(RTP)A 1999 and the need for reform.

MacMillan C, 'Upholding Contractual Intentions: Lord Denning's Dissent in *Scruttons Ltd v Midland Silicones Ltd* [1962] AC 446', in Geach N & Monaghan C (eds), *Dissenting Judgments in the Law* (Wildy, Simmonds & Hill, 2012) – Refer to this chapter for a discussion on *Scruttons Ltd* and Lord Denning's dissenting judgment.

Stone R, *The Modern Law of Contract*, 9th edn (Routledge, 2011) – Refer to this textbook for a more advanced consideration of the issues raised in this chapter.

Stone R, *Q&A Contract Law 2012–2013* (Routledge, 2012) – This book will help you to prepare for your exams.

COMPANION WEBSITE

An online glossary compiled by the authors is available on the companion website: www.routledge.com/cw/beginningthelaw

Chapter 9
Discharge of a contract

LEARNING OUTCOMES

After reading this chapter, you should be able to:

- Understand the different ways in which a contract can be discharged
- Appreciate the effect of the rule from *Cutter v Powell*
- Explain what is meant by an anticipatory breach
- Demonstrate knowledge of the rules on frustration of a contract
- Understand the remedies available upon frustration

WHAT IS MEANT BY DISCHARGE OF A CONTRACT?

Where a contract is discharged, the parties' obligations under the contract no longer exist; although, as we shall see, an action for breach of contract is still available after the contract has been discharged. In this chapter, we will see that a contract can be discharged in four ways. These are:

(i) Discharge by agreement
(ii) Discharge by performance
(iii) Discharge by breach
(iv) Discharge by frustration

DISCHARGE BY AGREEMENT

The parties can agree to discharge the contract. This operates where the obligations under the contract have not yet been performed, and the parties agree to waive contractual performance. The problem with discharge by agreement is that the promise to forgo performance must be supported by **consideration**. As we saw in Chapter 3, a promise to accept less (i.e. a promise to accept part payment of a debt owed) which has not been supported by consideration, will not be enforceable. Therefore, unless new consideration has been given, the party who has agreed to discharge the contract can, at a later date, demand that the other party performs their obligation. In these circumstances, the defendant might be able to rely upon promissory estoppel as a defence.

DISCHARGE BY PERFORMANCE

The contract can be discharged by performance. Most contracts are discharged in this way as the parties will both perform their contractual obligations and the contract will come to an end. This could operate where a builder has agreed to build an extension in return for payment upon completion of the work. Discharge by performance will take place when the extension is completed and the money has been paid.

Entire obligations rule

The case of *Cutter v Powell* (1795) 6 Term Reports 320 established the entire obligations rule.

KEY CASE ANALYSIS: *Cutter v Powell* (1795) 6 Term Reports 320

Background

Mrs Cutter sued a ship owner, Powell, to recover the wages of her late husband who had served as the second mate on the ship's voyage from Jamaica to Liverpool but had died halfway through the voyage. The ship owner had promised to pay 'Mr T Cutter the sum of 30 guineas, provided he proceeds, continues and does his duty as second mate in the said ship from hence to the port of Liverpool'.

Principle established

The court held that since Mr Cutter had died before completing his contractual obligations, his widow was not entitled to recover his wages under the contract or by way of quantum meruit (see Chapter 10, Remedies). The parties had to perform all their contractual obligations before the contract was discharged and they were entitled to payment.

The decision has been criticised by academics and judges, and the courts have provided exceptions to this harsh rule. However, it is important to appreciate why the court reached its decision. Ashurst J stated that the parties had agreed in their contract that the promise to pay depended on the entire performance of the contract by Mr Cutter. Grose J distinguished the contract between a divisible contract where you are paid monthly for your services, and the present contract where a large sum is paid for the entire completion of the contract. Lawrence J also distinguished the contract from an employment contract, where there was an implied understanding that employees are 'entitled to wages in proportion to the time they served'.

Exceptions to the entire obligations rule

The decision in *Cutter v Powell* has been applied in subsequent cases such as *Appleby v Myers* (1867) LR 2 CP 651. However, the courts have developed a number of exceptions to the entire obligations rule.

Substantial performance

The courts can hold that a contract has been discharged where a party has substantially performed their obligations. But what does substantial performance mean? The authors of *Anson's Law of Contract* state that substantial performance occurs where 'the actual performance falls not far short of the required performance, and if the cost of remedying the defects is not too great in amount in comparison with the contract price' (Beatson J *et al. Anson's Law of Contract* [29th edn, OUP, 2010], at p455). Substantial performance was used to pay a decorator for the work completed in *Hoenig v Issacs* [1952] 2 All ER 176, despite his failure to perform the entire contractual obligation of decorating the entire flat. In *Ministry of Sound (Ireland) Ltd v World Online Limited* [2003] EWHC 2178 (Ch), the claimants were attempting to recover an instalment of £200,000 that had been agreed in the contract. Sitting as a Deputy Judge, Mr Strauss QC doubted the existence of substantial performance, referring to it as the 'doubtful doctrine of substantial performance'. Importantly, substantial performance will only be available where there is an entire contract (i.e. an entire obligation).

According to Waller LJ in *SWI Ltd v P&I Data Services Ltd* [2007] EWCA Civ 663, substantial performance will only operate where the party seeking to recover payment is in breach of contract. Waller LJ stated that substantial performance 'enables a party with a fixed price to recover that price even though he may not have performed every item'. His Lordship stated that the theory is that the party should be able to recover the whole contract price minus a sum for the obligation that he has not performed.

Professor Peel has criticised the doctrine of substantial performance saying that it is 'based on the error that *contracts*, as opposed to particular *obligations*, can be entire . . . To say that an obligation is entire *means* that it must be completely performed before payment becomes due . . . In relation to 'entire' obligations, there is no scope for any doctrine of 'substantial performance'' (Peel, *Treitel on The Law of Contract* [12th edn, 2007] at para 17-03). Stevens and McFarlane support this view: 'It is submitted, however, that the leading textbook writers are correct to suggest that there is no room for the so-called doctrine of substantial performance. Obligations are entire, not contracts. The builder's obligation to complete the work was entire, his obligation to do so in a workmanlike manner was not' (LQR 200 11 [Oct], 569–99). Nonetheless, substantial performance is an important exception to entire obligation contracts where payment has not been made by instalments, but rather under a lump sum.

On-the-spot question

Is the exception of substantial performance justified?

Divisible contracts

Divisible contracts are contracts that can be divided into parts. After each part has been completed, the party who has performed it is entitled to payment. For example, courts will hold that employment contracts are divisible contracts and the employee will be entitled to be paid for the amount of work he has actually performed. In *Cutter v Powell* the courts held that this is an implied term in employment contracts, but because of the large sum payable to Mr Cutter, it was both parties' intention that the contract would not be divisible. According to the authors of *Chitty on Contracts*, 'In most modern contracts of any size, however, payments by instalments are specified, so that the law on entire obligations is not relevant to any obligation which has been completely performed' (30th edn, Vol 1, 21-029). Nonetheless, the courts will usually hold that where payment is payable as a lump sum, rather than in divisible instalments, there will be an implied term that there must be entire performance before the party performing is entitled to payment.

Acceptance of partial performance

Where a party has accepted the other party's partial performance, the party who has partially performed their contractual obligation may be able to recover part of the contract price for the work he has performed.

KEY CASE ANALYSIS: *Sumpter v Hedges* [1898] 1 QB 673

Background

A builder had agreed to build two houses and a stable for the defendant. The defendant in return had agreed to pay the builder a lump sum upon completion. The builder then announced that he was unable to finish the building work because he had run out of money. The builder sued the defendant to recover for the work he had done. The defendant had finished the building work, thus it was argued that the defendant had benefited from the claimant's work.

Principle established

The Court of Appeal refused to use quantum meruit to award the claimant a sum representing his work. Chitty LJ held that the claimant could recover where there was 'a fresh contract to pay for the work done', but with this fresh contract the court could not award *quantum meruit* as it would mean overruling *Cutter v Powell*.

So how then would a new contract arise? This was answered by Collins LJ who emphasised that the defendant needed to be given an option of whether to benefit from the work provided by the claimant. If the defendant had a choice and chose to benefit, there would be an inference of a new contract, but if there was no choice, such an inference would not exist.

The decision in *Sumpter v Hedges* has been criticised as unfair. However, it has been defended by Stevens and McFarlane, 'In defence of *Sumpter v Hedges* [2003] 118 LQR 569'.

Wrongful prevention

Where you have carried out work under an entire obligation contract and you are wrongfully prevented from completing the work by the other party, then you can recover a sum under *quantum meruit*. This remedy is designed to prevent unjust enrichment and is from the law of restitution. For an example of how this operates, see the decision in *Planché v Colburn* (1831) 8 Bing 14.

On-the-spot question

Sally asks Rupinda to help her produce a new range of books on wild animals. Rupinda is writing the book on hedgehogs. Please advise Rupinda as to her right to payment in the following alternative scenarios:

(i)   Rupinda has written half the book and has grown tired of writing it. She tells Sally that she will not write any more of the book and sends Sally what she has written. Sally finishes the book.
(ii) Rupinda has finished the book with the exception of the introduction and index. She is unable to complete these due to illness. She sends Sally what she has written.
(iii) Rupinda has written half the book and Sally has just informed her that the eminent zoologist Dr Zoo is now going to write the book, therefore Rupinda's version is no longer needed.

DISCHARGE BY BREACH

A contract can be discharged by a repudiatory breach of the contract by the defendant. It is important to note that not all breaches of contract will give the innocent party a right to repudiate the contract. Whether the innocent party can treat the defendant's breach of contract (i.e. failure to perform a contractual obligation) as allowing him to repudiate the contract and thus bring it to an end will depend on the classification of that contractual obligation (i.e. the term).

Key Definitions

- If a term is classified as a **condition**, upon breach of that term, the innocent party can choose to repudiate the contract and/or claim damages, or alternately choose to affirm the contract and claim damages.
- If a term is classified as a **warranty**, upon breach of that term, the innocent party can only claim damages. A breach of a warranty will never enable the innocent party to repudiate the contract.
- If a term is **innominate**, then the seriousness of the breach will determine whether the innocent party can repudiate the contract.

We are concerned here with repudiatory breaches of the contract. Affirmation of the contract will keep it alive and the parties' original contractual obligations will remain valid, thus the innocent party must still perform their own contractual obligations. Repudiation will discharge the contract and the contractual obligations will cease to exist. The innocent party will be able to recover damages for breach of contract.

Anticipatory breach

An anticipatory breach occurs where the defendant realises that he will be unable to perform his contractual obligations or he is unwilling to perform his contractual obligations and, in advance of the date required for performance, he informs the innocent party that he will be in breach of contract. The innocent party has two options: the first is to accept the breach and discharge the contract, and the second is to refuse to accept the breach and insist that the contract is performed. If the innocent party accepts the breach and the contract is discharged, then the innocent party can claim damages for breach of contract from the date of the anticipatory breach, and not from the date that the contractual performance was originally due.

So why insist that the defendant fulfils the contract? The reason is that the innocent party can recover the entire contract price without having to mitigate their losses. We can see how this operates from the important decisions in *Hochster v De La Tour* (1853) 2 E & B 678 and *White and Carter (Councils) Ltd v McGregor* [1962] AC 413.

KEY CASE ANALYSIS: *White and Carter (Councils) Ltd v McGregor* [1962] AC 413

Background

The claimant had contracted with the defendant to advertise its garage on the claimant's litter bins for three years. The defendant immediately informed the claimant that they had made a mistake and no longer wished to advertise. The claimant refused to accept the anticipatory breach, and five months later, in accordance with the contract, began to advertise the defendant's garages on its litter bins. They sought to do this to recover the contract price, rather than having to mitigate their losses by finding alternative parties to advertise.

Principle established

The majority of the House of Lords held that the claimant could recover the full contract price. Lord Reid stated that:

> If one party to a contract repudiates it in the sense of making it clear to the other party that he refuses or will refuse to carry out his part of the contract, the other party, the innocent party, has an option. He may accept that repudiation and sue for damages for breach of contract, whether or not the time for performance has come; or he may if he chooses disregard or refuse to accept it and then the contract remains in full effect . . .

> It may well be that, if it can be shown that a person has no legitimate interest, financial or otherwise, in performing the contract rather than claiming damages, he ought not to be allowed to saddle the other party with an additional burden with no benefit to himself. If a party has no interest to enforce a stipulation, he cannot in general enforce it: so it might be said that, if a party has no interest to insist on a particular remedy, he ought not to be allowed to insist on it.

Looking at Lord Reid's judgment it is clear that a party who has a legitimate interest in performing the contract, as opposed to claiming damages, can insist that the contract is performed. Therefore, the defendant must prove to the court that the innocent party does not have a legitimate interest in performing the contract. The defendant in *White & Carter* did not attempt to do this, as Lord Reid acknowledged. Lord Reid recognises that where there is no legitimate interest it is pointless to impose a burden on the defendant where there is no benefit to the innocent party in performing the contract. Crucially, the innocent party should not require the defendant's co-operation in performing the contract. Therefore, if you require the defendant's co-operation (i.e. access to their premises to carry out the work), you will be unable to refuse to accept their breach. For an interesting discussion on *White & Carter* see Liu Q, 'The White and Carter Principle: A Restatement' [2011] 74(2) MLR 171.

DISCHARGE BY FRUSTRATION

A contract is frustrated where an event that occurs after contracting renders performance of the obligations under the contract impossible, illegal or radically different. Where a contract is deemed to have been frustrated, the obligations under the contract no longer need to be performed and the contract is discharged. The **doctrine of frustration** has been very narrowly applied by the courts since they are keen to preserve the principle of freedom of contract and so are unwilling to allow the parties to a contract to simply escape a bad bargain. Historically, the concept of frustration was not recognised (see *Paradine v Jane* (1647) 82 ER 519), but in more recent years, the doctrine of frustration has developed to allow the parties to escape from a contract where the obligations under it cannot be performed due to an unforeseeable event. Nevertheless, this doctrine has developed under strict rules, which has ensured that the doctrine is only narrowly applied in rare circumstances. As Lord Radcliffe stated in *Davis Contractors Ltd v Fareham Urban District Council* [1956] AC 696, '. . . in my opinion, full weight ought to be given to the requirement that the parties "must have made" their bargain on the particular footing. Frustration is not to be lightly invoked as the dissolvent of a contract'.

By contrast, ***force majeure*** clauses operate in much wider contractual settings. These are clauses that are incorporated into a contract and provide for the discharge of a contract or the delay to the performance of contractual obligations upon the occurrence of an event. The courts are much more willing to allow for the operation of *force majeure* clauses since these have been agreed by both parties upon contracting and thus are consistent with the principle of freedom of contract.

Key Definitions

Doctrine of frustration – A contract is frustrated where an event that occurs after contracting renders performance of the obligations under the contract impossible, illegal or radically different.

> ***Force majeure* clause** – A clause in a contract that provides for the discharge of the contract or for delay to the performance of contractual obligations upon the occurrence of an event.

The doctrine of frustration operates to discharge the obligations under a contract where an event takes place that renders performance of those obligations impossible, illegal or radically different to those that were agreed to at the time of contracting.

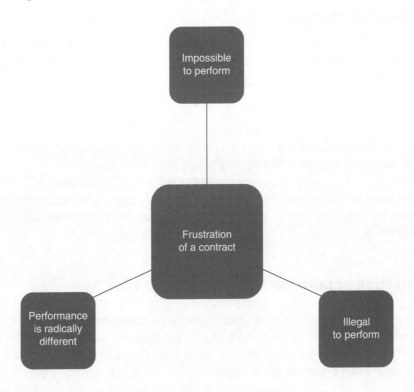

Impossibility

Where it becomes impossible for one of the parties to a contract to perform their obligations under the contract, the contract is frustrated.

KEY CASE ANALYSIS: *Taylor v Caldwell* (1863) 3 B&S 826

Background

This case involved a contract for the hire of a music hall and gardens for a concert. After contracting but before the actual day of the concert, the music hall was accidentally destroyed by a fire. The claimant sued the defendant for breach of contract (for failing to provide the music hall for the concert as per his obligations under the contract) and sought to recover damages to cover his expenses.

Principle established

It was held that the fire had rendered it impossible for the defendant to perform his obligations under the contract, and therefore the contract was discharged by frustration.

Where the subject matter of the contract is totally destroyed, rendering performance impossible, the contract will be frustrated. The case of *Taylor v Caldwell* also demonstrates that partial destruction of the subject matter may also frustrate a contract, provided that performance is rendered impossible by the destruction. In this case, only the music hall was destroyed and not the gardens, but performance was still impossible.

Frustration of purpose

Where an unforeseeable event occurs that affects the purpose of the contract, so that the obligations under it can no longer be performed, the contract is frustrated. Frustration of the purpose of the contract is relatively rare. There are two key cases, which are factually similar but in which the courts reached opposite conclusions as to whether the contract was frustrated or not. These are often referred to as the 'Coronation cases' since their facts relate to the Coronation of King Edward VII, which was unexpectedly postponed after the King became ill.

On-the-spot question

 Read the summary of the two cases below and compare the facts and decisions. Why do you think that the courts reached the opposite conclusions in these cases? Can these cases be reconciled?

KEY CASE ANALYSIS: *Krell v Henry* [1903] 2 KB 740

Background

The defendant in this case contracted to hire a flat in Pall Mall from the plaintiff (claimant) on the days (but not the nights) on which the Coronation processions were due to pass down Pall Mall. The defendant's purpose in hiring the flat was to watch the processions from it, although this was not expressly referred to in the contract itself. He paid a deposit for the hire of the flat upon contracting. The processions were postponed and the defendant refused to pay the outstanding balance owed for the hire of the flat.

Principle established

The Court of Appeal held that it could be inferred that both parties recognised that the purpose of the contract was the Coronation processions and that this was regarded by both parties as the foundation of the contract. The postponement of the processions was an event unforeseen by both parties, and thus the contract for hire was frustrated and the defendant did not have to pay the balance owed for the hire of the flat.

Vaughan Williams LJ stated that:

> . . . the use of the rooms was let and taken for the purpose of seeing the Royal procession. [This] was regarded by both contracting parties as the foundation of the contract . . . the rooms were offered and taken, by reason of their peculiar suitability from the position of the rooms for a view of the coronation procession, surely the view of the coronation procession was the foundation of the contract . . . In each case one must ask oneself, first, what, having regard to all the circumstances, was the foundation of the contract? Secondly, was the performance of the contract prevented? Thirdly, was the event which prevented the performance of the contract of such a character that it cannot reasonably be said to have been in the contemplation of the parties at the date of the contract? If all these questions are answered in the affirmative (as I think they should be in this case), I think both parties are discharged from further performance of the contract.

KEY CASE ANALYSIS: *Herne Bay Steam Boat Co v Hutton* [1903] 2 KB 683

Background

In this case, the defendant chartered the plaintiff's steamship on the dates of the Royal naval review, which was due to be held in celebration of the King's Coronation. The contract stated that the purpose of the contract was to view the naval review and for a day's cruise around the fleet. The defendant paid a deposit upon contracting and the balance was due to be paid before the steamship left Herne Bay. As a result of the King's illness, the naval review was cancelled. The defendant did not turn up on the scheduled days to take the ship out and the plaintiffs used the ship themselves and made a profit. They then sued the defendant to recover the balance owed under the contract, minus the profits that they made by using the ship on the days that it had been due to be hired to the defendant.

Principle established

The Court of Appeal held that the plaintiffs were able to recover the money owed (minus the profits) because the naval review was not the sole purpose of the contract, so the contract was not frustrated. Vaughan Williams LJ held that there were two objectives of the defendant in hiring the ship: the first was taking people to see the naval review, and the second was to take people to see the fleet. The Court held that in this case there was not a total failure of consideration, nor was there a total destruction of the subject matter of the contract. Stirling LJ stated that the defendant's purpose was to make a profit from paying customers and that he bore the risk in this venture alone.

Vaughan Williams LJ:

> I see nothing that makes this contract differ from a case where, for instance, a person has engaged a brake to take himself and a party to Epsom to see the races there, but for some reason or other, such as the spread of an infectious disease, the races are postponed. In such a case it could not be said that he could be relieved of his bargain. So in the present case it is sufficient to say that the happening of the naval review was not the foundation of the contract.

Stirling LJ:

> ... the object of the voyage is not limited to the naval review, but also extends to a cruise round the fleet. The fleet was there, and passengers

> might have been found willing to go round it. It is true that in the event
> which happened, the object of the voyage became limited, but, in my
> opinion, that was the risk of the defendant whose venture the taking the
> passengers was.

Illegality

Where, after contracting, there is a change in the law that would render performance of the obligations under the contract illegal, the contract is frustrated. This principle is supported by the House of Lords' authority, *Denny, Mott & Dickinson Ltd v James B Fraser & Co Ltd* [1944] AC 265. In this case, a trading agreement was entered into between timber merchants prior to the Second World War. After the outbreak of the war, war regulations were introduced that restricted transactions in timber and effectively rendered the performance of the obligations under the contract illegal. It was held that the war regulations operated to frustrate the contract. Similarly, in the earlier case of *Metropolitan Water Board v Dick Kerr & Co Ltd* [1918] AC 119, the defendants contracted to build a reservoir for the plaintiffs within six years. However, the Ministry of Munitions exercised statutory powers to prohibit work on the contract. The defendants claimed that the performance of contract had become illegal and impossible by the notice issued by the Minister of Munitions, and that, consequently, the contract was discharged by frustration. The House of Lords agreed that the contract was frustrated.

Radically different

As stated above, where a supervening event, which occurs after the contract is made but before performance of the obligations under it, renders performance of those obligations radically different to what was contemplated by the parties at the time of contracting, the contract is also frustrated. The leading authority on this point is *Davis Contractors Ltd v Fareham Urban District Council* [1956] AC 696.

KEY CASE ANALYSIS: *Davis Contractors Ltd v Fareham Urban District Council* [1956] AC 696

Background

This case involved a building contract due to last eight months, which both parties entered into on the basis that supplies of labour and materials would be available at the required times. However, due to unexpected circumstances that were the fault of neither party, adequate supplies were not available, which meant that the building project was delayed and took an additional 14 months to complete.

Principle established

The House of Lords held that the contract was not frustrated by mere delay and additional cost. While a contract can be frustrated where a supervening event renders performance of the obligations under a contract 'radically different', this means that the performance of the obligations after the supervening event must be *something different* to that which was contemplated at the time of contracting. Where the event merely makes the obligations under the contract *more onerous* to perform, the contract is not frustrated. Lord Radcliffe stated that:

> . . . frustration occurs whenever the law recognises that without default of either party a contractual obligation has become incapable of being performed because the circumstances in which performance is called for would render it a thing radically different from that which was undertaken by the contract.

> . . . it is not hardship or inconvenience or material loss itself which calls the principle of frustration into play. There must be as well such a change in the significance of the obligation that the thing undertaken would, if performed, be a different thing from that contracted for.

Thus, a contract may only be frustrated where the obligations under it become something different to what was originally agreed. It is not enough that it will merely take longer, or more effort or more money to perform the obligations under the contract. In *Amalgamated Investment & Property Co v John Walker & Sons* (1975) 235 EG 565, it was confirmed that where a supervening event meant that the performance of the contract was economically less advantageous, the contract was not frustrated.

Contracts for personal services

A contract may also be frustrated where the contract is for personal services, such as a contract of employment, and the personal service is unavailable due to death or incapacity. In *Condor v The Barron Knights Ltd* [1966] 1 WLR 87, a musical band employed a drummer to play in their band on the basis that he should be available to perform seven nights a week. The drummer fell ill and a doctor advised that he should not perform on more than four nights a week. The band fired the drummer and the drummer sued the band for wrongful dismissal. It was held that it was impossible for the drummer to continue to perform in accordance with his contractual obligations, so the dismissal was not wrongful. This case serves as an example of frustration of a contract for personal services by illness.

Similarly, in *FC Shepherd & Co Ltd v Jerrom* [1987] QB 301, the Court of Appeal held that an employment contract could be frustrated by the imprisonment of the employee. In this case, an apprentice plumber had a four-year apprenticeship contract. He was convicted of criminal offences and sentenced to six months' imprisonment. His employers were not prepared to take the apprentice back, so he sued them for wrongful dismissal. The employers argued that there had been no dismissal, but rather the contract had been frustrated by the sentence of imprisonment, but this was rejected at first instance by the Industrial Tribunal and this decision was upheld by the Employment Appeal Tribunal. However, the Court of Appeal held that the sentence of imprisonment was an unforeseeable event and it rendered performance of the contract radically different from that which the parties contemplated at the time of contracting; and in this case, the sentence of imprisonment did frustrate the apprenticeship contract.

Leases

Historically, it was not possible to frustrate a lease (see *Paradine v Jane* (1647) 82 ER 519), but more recently it has been held that a lease may be frustrated in exceptional circumstances (according to *National Carriers Ltd v Panalpina (Northern) Ltd* [1981] AC 675). In simple terms, a lease is a contract for the use of a property and/or land. There is a large variety of different types of lease: the leasehold of a flat can be purchased and might last for 125 years; alternatively, a person might rent a flat on a short-term lease for just a week or two. Professor Ewan McKendrick comments that while long leases that run for many years are unlikely to be frustrated, short leases might be: '[t]he type of lease which might be frustrated is a lease of a holiday flat or some other lease of short duration' (*Contract Law* [9th edn, Palgrave, 2011] at p258).

Foreseeability

There are further limitations to the doctrine of frustration which ensure that the operation of the doctrine is kept under narrow confines. The first requires that the supervening event must not have been in the contemplation of the parties at the time of contracting (i.e. it must have been unforeseen).

Self-induced frustration

The second further limitation is that the frustrating event must not have been induced by the party seeking to rely on frustration; thus frustration cannot be self-induced. Where the supervening event has been brought about by the party seeking to escape performance by frustration, the doctrine of frustration will not operate and the obligations under the contract are not discharged. This was confirmed by the Privy Council in *Maritime National Fish Ltd v Ocean Trawlers Ltd* [1935] AC 524, where it was held that where the supervening event was as a result of a choice made by one of the parties, it was within their control, and thus the contract would not be frustrated. This strict approach is applied by the courts even where the party in question has not acted negligently or breached the contract. In *J Lauritzen AS v Wijsmuller BV (The Super Servant Two)* [1990] 1 Lloyd's Rep 1, the Court of Appeal held that where a party voluntarily makes a decision that is then causatively linked to the supervening event, there is no frustration. So in this case, the defendants had contracted to transport an oil rig for the plaintiffs using a specified vessel. However, the defendants later decided to use a different vessel (the Super Servant Two) for the transportation, which sank. The defendants claimed that the contract was frustrated by the sinking of the vessel, but the Court of Appeal held that the doctrine of frustration could not operate since it had been the defendant's decision to use the different vessel, and thus the frustration was self-induced.

Financial consequences

Where a contract is frustrated, the obligations under the contract are discharged. Under the old common law, this meant that while any money due to be paid after the date of the frustrating event was no longer payable, any money paid prior to the date of the frustrating event in accordance with the contract could not be recovered in the event of frustration, and it remained payable if not already paid (*Chandler v Webster* [1904] 1 KB 493). However, in *Fibrosa Spolka Akcyjna v Fairbairn Lawson Combe Barbour Ltd* [1943] AC 32, the House of Lords held that money already paid could be recovered where there was a total failure of consideration (i.e. where the other party had provided no consideration in return).

The Law Reform (Frustrated Contracts) Act 1943 significantly reformed the law in relation to money paid or payable prior to the date of the frustrating event. Under s 1(2), any money paid or payable before the date of the frustrating event is recoverable, or if it is yet to be paid, ceases to be payable. Section 1(2) states that:

> All sums paid or payable to any party in pursuance of the contract before the time when the parties were so discharged (in this Act referred to as 'the time of discharge') shall, in the case of sums so paid, be recoverable from him as money received by him for the use of the party by whom the sums were paid, and, in the case of sums so payable, cease to be so payable:

> Provided that, if the party to whom the sums were so paid or payable incurred expenses before the time of discharge in, or for the purpose of, the performance of the contract, the court may, if it considers it just to do so having regard to all

the circumstances of the case, allow him to retain or, as the case may be, recover the whole or any part of the sums so paid or payable, not being an amount in excess of the expenses so incurred.

Where money was not owed or paid prior to the frustrating event, but where one party obtains a valuable benefit prior to the date of the frustrating event, s 1(3), Law Reform (Frustrated Contracts) Act 1943 provides that the court has the discretion to award the other party a sum of money that it considers just having regard to the circumstances of the case. This provision was considered by Goff J in *BP Exploration Co (Libya) Ltd v Hunt (No 2)* [1979] 1 WLR 783. In this case, Goff J stated that the court should identify the valuable benefit that has been conferred on the other party and place a value upon this. That value would then be the maximum sum of money that the court can award. The court should then decide what sum it would be just to award (up to the maximum) in the circumstances of the case.

Under both ss 1(2) and 1(3), the court has the discretion to deduct a sum to cover any expenditure incurred by the party to whom the money had been paid or was payable. The sum deducted must not exceed the amount of the expenses incurred and the test to be applied is whether the court considers it 'just' to deduct a sum having regard to the circumstances of the case (see *Gamerco SA v ICM/Fair Warning (Agency) Ltd* [1995] 1 WLR 1226).

SUMMARY

- The contract can be discharged by performance of the parties' contractual obligations. Prior to performance the parties can agree to discharge the contract, but this agreement will be unenforceable unless consideration is provided.
- A repudiatory breach will enable the innocent party to choose to discharge the contract. The parties' contract obligations will cease and the defendant will have to pay damages.
- A contract can be discharged by frustration where the contract becomes impossible or illegal or radically different to perform. Frustration will not occur where the frustrating event makes the contract merely more expensive to perform, or where the event is foreseeable or self-induced.
- The Law Reform (Frustrated Contracts) Act 1943 has reformed the law relating to the recovery of money paid before the frustrating event occurred.

FURTHER READING

Liu Q, 'The White and Carter Principle: A Restatement' [2011] 74(2) MLR 171 – This article reassesses the decision in the key House of Lords decision.

McElroy RG and Williams G, 'The Coronation Cases – I' [1941] (4) MLR 240 – This article looks at the case of *Krell v Henry* and the inability to discharge a lease using frustration. The authors take the view that the doctrine of frustration should not apply to cases such as *Krell v Henry*.

McElroy RG and Williams G, 'The Coronation Cases – II' [1941] (5) MLR 20 – This article looks at the case of *Chandler v Webster* and the proposals for reforming the rules on the return of money (now the Law Reform (Frustrated Contracts) Act 1943).

Parker M and McKendrick E, 'Drafting force majeure clauses: some practical considerations' [2000] 11(4) ICCLR 132 – This article looks at the use of *force majeure* clauses and their relationship with common law frustration.

Stevens R and McFarlane B, 'In defence of *Sumpter v Hedges*' [2003] 118 LQR 569 – This article is recommended reading because it looks at the exceptions to the entire obligation rule. It is extremely interesting and defends the decision in *Sumpter v Hedges*, and criticises the use of substantial performance as an exception to *Cutter v Powell*.

Stone R, *The Modern Law of Contract*, 9th edn (Routledge, 2011) – Refer to this textbook for a more advanced exploration of the issues raised in this chapter.

Stone R, *Q&A Contract Law 2012–2013* (Routledge, 2012) – This book will help you to prepare for your exams.

COMPANION WEBSITE

An online glossary compiled by the authors is available on the companion website: www.routledge.com/cw/beginningthelaw

Chapter 10
Remedies

LEARNING OUTCOMES

After reading this chapter, you should be able to:

- Understand the different remedies available to a wronged party in the law of contract
- Explain the difference between expectation interest and reliance interest
- Appreciate the limitations on recovering expectation interest
- Outline the test for remoteness in contract law
- Demonstrate knowledge of the various equitable remedies available

DAMAGES

Where a claimant successfully sues another in the law of contract, the most common remedy available to compensate the claimant is an award of **damages**. For instance, we have already seen that damages are available to compensate a claimant where the other party has breached a term of their contract, or where one party makes a misrepresentation to the other contracting party that induces that party to enter into the contract. An award of damages is available as a common law remedy and damages will be awarded unless the court considers that it is inappropriate to do so.

The aim of an award of damages is to compensate the claimant for the loss that they have suffered and the normal measure of damages in contract law seeks to put the claimant in the position that they would have been in had the contract been performed. Thus, damages in contract law look ahead to the position that the claimant would have been in after performance of the obligations under the contract and protect the claimant's **expectation interest**. As Parker B stated in *Robinson v Harman* (1848) 1 Exch 850, '[w]here a party sustains a loss by reason of a breach of contract he is, so far as money can do it, to be placed in the same situation with respect to damages as if the contract had been performed'. Although the normal aim of damages in contract law is to protect the expectation interest of the claimant, there are a number of limitations on recovering the expectation interest that are outlined in the next section. If the expectation interest is not recoverable, then the claimant may instead recover damages that seek to put the claimant back in the position that they were in prior to entering into the contract. This measure of damages takes the claimant back to their pre-contractual position and protects the **reliance interest** of the claimant.

Key Definitions

Expectation interest – Seeking to put the claimant in the position that they would have been in had the contract been performed.

Reliance interest – Seeking to put the claimant back in the position that they were in prior to entering into the contract.

LIMITATIONS ON RECOVERING EXPECTATION INTEREST

Unquantifiable

A claimant will not be able to recover his expectation losses where those losses are too difficult to quantify. So, where a claimant is unable to calculate exactly how much money he would have had had the contract been performed (expectation losses), a different measure of damages must be adopted (reliance losses). An example of a case in which the expectation losses were unquantifiable is the case of *Anglia Television Ltd v Reed* [1972] 1 QB 60.

KEY CASE ANALYSIS: *Anglia Television Ltd v Reed* [1972] 1 QB 60

Background

In this case, Anglia Television had contracted with a famous television actor, Mr Reed, who was due to star in a film that they were producing. However, Mr Reed changed his mind about appearing in the film before the filming began. Anglia Television sued Mr Reed for breach of contract. The issue was whether they were entitled to damages under the expectation or reliance interest.

Principal established

The court held that Anglia Television could only recover damages under the reliance interest. This was because it was impossible for Anglia Television to calculate the expectation losses as they could not quantify their expected profits had Mr Reed starred in the film. So they could not recover their expectation losses, but were limited to recovering only their reliance losses (which put the claimants back in the position that they were in before entering into the contract), such as any expenses incurred in preparation for filming that were reasonably within the contemplation of the parties.

Another example of a case in which the expectation losses were unquantifiable is the case of *McRae v Commonwealth Disposal Commission* (1951) 84 CLR 377, in which the claimants sought to recover damages in respect of a wrecked oil tanker that they purchased from the defendants and that they later discovered did not exist. The defendants were deemed to have assumed the risk in guaranteeing the existence of the tanker, but in this case it was impossible to quantify the claimants' expectation losses (the potential loss of profits) since the tanker and oil supplies did not in fact ever exist. So, the claimants were awarded their reliance losses, to cover the money spent on searching for the tanker.

Cost of cure disproportionate

A claimant will also be unable to recover his expectation losses where the court considers those to be disproportionate to the breach of contract. This is demonstrated in the case of *Ruxley Electronics and Construction Ltd v Forsyth* [1996] AC 344. This case involved a contract for the construction of a swimming pool in the defendant's garden. The claimants contracted to build a pool that ran to a depth of 7 feet 6 inches in the diving area. However, after construction the pool was only 6 foot deep in the diving area. To ensure that the defendant was placed in the position that he expected to be in had the contract been performed properly (to calculate his expectation losses), the cost of fixing the problem by rebuilding the pool so that the diving area reached the depth contracted for (the 'cost of cure') was calculated at £21,560. However, the House of Lords was unwilling to allow the defendant to recover such an excessive and disproportionate sum of money in light of the fact that the defendant had been supplied with a pool that was suitable for domestic use. Consequently, the House held that the defendant had only really suffered disappointment and awarded him the sum of £2,500 for loss of amenity.

On-the-spot question

? Music Corp manages Tiny Y, an up-and-coming singer. On Tiny Y's debut album, Music Corp secures the world famous, multimillion-record-selling artist, Jimmy J, to duet on one track. This is intended to be released as Tiny Y's debut single and is expected to get a lot of radio air-play. After contracting, Jimmy J realises that he will be much too busy and informs Music Corp that he will be unable to duet with Tiny Y.

Advise Music Corp.

Remoteness

The innocent party will only be able to recover any damages in compensation which are not too remote from the loss.

KEY CASE ANALYSIS: *Hadley v Baxendale* (1854) 156 ER 145

Background

The crankshaft of a mill had broken and Hadley could not use the mill without it. Hadley contracted with Baxendale to supply a replacement crankshaft. Hadley stated that it needed to be delivered immediately and Baxendale promised to deliver it the following day; however, he did not deliver the crankshaft until seven days later. Hadley sought to recover damages for the five days that the mill could not be used. The issue was whether Hadley's damages would be too remote.

Principle established

The court held that the damages were not too remote. The test for remoteness was established by Alderson B, who stated that:

> Where two parties have made a contract which one of them has broken, the damages which the other party ought to receive in respect of such breach of contract should be such as may fairly and reasonably be considered either arising naturally, i.e., according to the usual course of things, from such breach of contract itself, or such as may reasonably be supposed to have been in the contemplation of both parties, at the time they made the contract, as the probable result of the breach of it.

Applying this test, Hadley was entitled to recover the lost profits for five days, because the damages arose naturally from Baxendale's breach of contract and, additionally, it should have been in the parties' contemplation that the crankshaft was required to operate the mill and any delay would prevent the mill from being used.

There are two parts to this test. The first part allows a claimant to recover any damages that arise naturally from the breach of contract. Alternatively, the second part allows a claimant to recover any damages that ought reasonably to have been contemplated by both parties at the time of contracting. This means that the claimant will not be able to recover where the damages do not arise naturally out of the breach of contract, or where the damages were not within the reasonable contemplation of both parties at the time of contracting. The test can be explained with reference to the decision in *Victoria Laundry (Windsor) v Newman Industries* [1949] 2 KB 528.

KEY CASE ANALYSIS: *Victoria Laundry (Windsor) v Newman Industries* **[1949] 2 KB 528**

Background

In this case the defendant had contracted to supply and install a boiler for the claimant, the owner of the laundry. Unfortunately, the defendant damaged the boiler and this resulted in a long delay before the defendant could deliver the boiler to the claimant's premises. The claimants sued the defendants for breach of contract and tried to recover their loss of profits, which could be broken down into two parts:

1. Regular business; and
2. A highly lucrative dyeing contract for the Ministry of Supply

Principle established

The Court of Appeal held that the claimants could only recover for the losses from their regular business, because this flowed naturally from the breach. This was recoverable under the first part of the test from *Hadley v Baxendale*. The highly lucrative dyeing contract for the Ministry of Supply could not be recovered under the first part, because it was a special loss that did not arise naturally from the breach. Neither could the claimant recover this special loss under the second test, because the defendants could not reasonably have contemplated that there would be such a lucrative contract at time of contracting.

In 2008, in *Transfield Shipping Inc v Mercator Shipping Inc (The Achilleas)* [2008] UKHL 48, the House of Lords limited the recovery of losses by adopting a stricter approach to remoteness.

Mitigating the claimant's losses

The claimant must take reasonable steps to mitigate his losses. He is expected to avoid doing anything that will make his losses worse, but he is not expected to go to extreme lengths to reduce his losses; he need only take reasonable steps to minimise the extent of his losses (see *British Westinghouse Co v Underground Electric Railway Co* [1912] AC 673). If a coach company hires out a coach to the defendant who then breaches the contract by announcing he no longer needs the coach, the coach company is expected to take reasonable steps to hire out the coach to other parties. He is not expected to do anything more than what a normal or prudent commercial party would do in the circumstances.

On-the-spot question

In the above example, involving the contract to hire a coach, what steps would you expect the claimant to take in order to mitigate his losses?

EQUITABLE REMEDIES

In contract law, the normal remedy for breach of contract is damages. The courts can also award equitable remedies, but these are discretionary and the normal rule is that equitable remedies will only be awarded where damages would be inappropriate.

Specific performance

If the defendant breaches the contract, the courts will normally award damages to the claimant, and will not compel the defendant to perform the contract. Specific performance is an equitable remedy and is awarded by the court where damages would not be appropriate. In contracts for the sale of goods where damages are not an adequate remedy, the courts can award specific performance where there is a contract for specific or ascertained goods (s 52, Sale of Goods Act 1979). In *Behnke v Bede Shipping Co* [1927] 1 KB 649, the court awarded specific performance because the buyer could not obtain a similar ship elsewhere and required a ship of that specification in order to use it in Germany.

Injunctions

An injunction is an equitable remedy that is awarded at the discretion of the court. It is a court order that will prevent someone from acting in a particular way, such as breaching a contract. The courts will only award an injunction where damages would not be an appropriate remedy.

RESTITUTIONARY REMEDIES

Restitutionary remedies are intended to prevent the defendant from being unjustly enriched.

Quantum meruit

Quantum meruit is a restitutionary remedy and can be awarded by the courts after the contract has ended, or where a contract has never existed between the parties. The purpose of *quantum meruit* is to avoid the defendant from being unjustly enriched at the claimant's expense. A case that illustrates when *quantum meruit* can be recovered is *British Steel Corporation v Cleveland Bridge & Engineering Co Ltd* [1984] 1 All ER 504. Here the defendant had asked the claimant to begin work before they had formally entered into the contract. However, the negotiations between the parties broke down, and since there was no contract between the parties, the claimant successfully sued the defendant to recover his losses under *quantum meruit*. The defendant had to pay a reasonable sum towards the cost of the goods manufactured because they had been manufactured at their request. More recently, the Court of Appeal in *Whittle Loves Ltd v Hollywood Express Ltd* [2009] EWCA Civ 1189 applied *British Steel Corporation* and held that where the parties were negotiating, it would be unlikely that there would be a contract between them, and where there was no contract the remedy would be *quantum meruit* and not contractual damages.

Account of profits

Where the defendant has made a profit by breaching the contract, the claimant may ask the court for the remedy of restitution. Its purpose is to prevent the defendant from being unjustly enriched at the expense of the claimant, and it is an attractive remedy where the defendant's gain greatly exceeds the claimant's damages. Prior to the House of Lords' decision in *Attorney-General v Blake* [2001] 1 AC 268, the ability to claim restitution for breach of contract was very limited. George Blake was 'a notorious, self-confessed traitor' who defected to the Russians during the Cold War. He wrote a memoir and breached his contract with the security services. The government sued Blake and sought to recover all profits from the book. The House of Lords allowed the restitutionary remedy of account of profits. It was held that this remedy would only be awarded in exceptional circumstances, where damages would not be the appropriate remedy. Lord Nicholls noted that: 'Most writers have favoured the view that in some circumstances the innocent party to a breach of contract should be able to compel the defendant to disgorge the profits he obtained from his breach of contract. However, there is a noticeable absence of any consensus on what are the circumstances in which this remedy should be available' (at p278). The House of Lords held that the government had a legitimate interest to prevent Blake from breaching his contract, because publication of the book was not in the public interest. Lord Nicholls was clear that allowing recovery for account of profits should not be the norm: 'I must also sound a further note of warning that if some more extensive principle of awarding non-compensatory damages for breach of contract is to be introduced into our commercial law, the consequences will be very far reaching and disruptive.' We can see that Lord Nicholls issues this warning because, otherwise, commercial parties will choose to breach a contract for commercial reasons (i.e. to obtain a better contract price elsewhere).

On-the-spot question

 Why did Lord Nicholls in *Attorney-General v Blake* warn against awarding account of profits in commercial disputes?

PENALTY CLAUSES

The parties can choose to include a clause in the contract that specifies a sum of money to be paid to the innocent in the event of breach of contract. This is known as a **liquidated damages clause**. Such clauses are valid so long as the sum payable is a reasonable pre-estimate of the innocent party's loss at the time of contracting. However, where the sum is not a genuine pre-estimate of the innocent party's loss, it is known as a **penalty clause**. Penalty clauses are not valid because they are intended to compel performance, rather than to compensate the innocent party.

KEY CASE ANALYSIS: *Dunlop Pneumatic Tyre Co Ltd v New Garage and Motor Co Ltd* [1915] AC 79

Background

In this case the claimants were manufacturers and had contracted to sell the defendants' motor tyres. The defendants had agreed in the contract not to tamper with the marks on the goods and not to resell the goods on to third parties below list price. Every time the defendants breached the contract, they had agreed to pay a sum of 5l. The issue was whether the sum due was a liquidated damages clause or a penalty clause.

Principle established

Lord Dunedin establishes rules for distinguishing between a liquidated damages clause and a penalty clause. His Lordship stated that the test to be used was whether the money payable was too great in comparison with the claimants' actual losses. The time for calculating what the claimants' likely losses were would be a time of contracting. If the sum due under the clause was too great, then the clause would be a penalty clause and thus invalid. The courts would then proceed to calculate the claimants' actual losses.

SUMMARY

- Where there has been a breach of contract, the innocent party will be entitled to damages. The usual measure of damages will be recovery under the expectation interest. The innocent party will only be able to recover damages that are not too remote and is expected to mitigate his losses.
- Equitable remedies are awarded at the discretion of the courts and will be awarded where damages are an inappropriate remedy.

FURTHER READING

Bridge M, 'Mitigation of damages in contract and the meaning of avoidable loss' (1989) 105 LQR 398 – This article explores the theoretical basis of the duty to mitigate loss and focuses on the extent to which a party is required to enter into a new contract with the defendant upon discharge of the contract by the defendant's breach.

Cooke R, 'Remoteness of damages and judicial discretion' [1978] 37 CLJ 288 – This article considers the law on remoteness in both contract and tort. It provides a detailed and valuable analysis of the leading authorities on remoteness, such as *Hadley v Baxendale*, *Victoria Laundry (Windsor) Ltd v Newman Industries Ltd* and *Parsons v Uttley Ingham & Co*, as well as other cases on remoteness.

Coote B, 'Contract damages, *Ruxley* and the performance interest' [1997] CLJ 537 – In this paper, the author considers the case of *Ruxley Electronics Ltd v Forsyth*, and explores the different judicial opinions existing in relation to law of damages. He argues that protecting the performance interest in a contract should be the primary objective of an award of damages.

Friedmann D, 'The performance interest in contract damages' [1995] 111 LQR 628 – In this article, the author challenges an article written in 1936, which favours the reliance interest as a measure of damages in contract law. This article, by Professor Friedmann, examines the difficulty with that approach and advocates instead the application of the performance interest in contract law.

Robertson A, 'The basis of the remoteness rule in contract' (2008) Legal Studies 172 – This article challenges the view that the concept of remoteness is used to discover where the contracting parties implicitly agreed to allocate risk, but argues instead that case law demonstrates that the remoteness rule provides the courts with a method to allocate risk where the parties have in fact failed to do so, and thus, it acts as a 'gap-filling' mechanism.

COMPANION WEBSITE

An online glossary compiled by the authors is available on the companion website: www.routledge.com/cw/beginningthelaw

Index